Make It Plant-Based!
Indian

Make It Plant-Based!

Indian

50+ RECIPES FOR VEGAN CURRIES, CHAAT, BREAKFASTS, BREADS, AND SWEETS

Srishti Jain

Mehreen Karim, series editor

Photographs by Emma Fishman

WORKMAN PUBLISHING • NEW YORK

Workman
Workman Publishing
Hachette Book Group, Inc.
1290 Avenue of the Americas
New York, NY 10104
workman.com

Workman is an imprint of Workman Publishing, a division of Hachette Book Group, Inc. The Workman name and logo are registered trademarks of Hachette Book Group, Inc.

Design by Suet Chong
Cover illustration by str33t cat/Shutterstock, Inc.

The publisher is not responsible for websites (or their content) that are not owned by the publisher.

Workman books may be purchased in bulk for business, educational, or promotional use. For information, please contact your local bookseller or the Hachette Book Group Special Markets Department at special.markets@hbgusa.com.

Library of Congress Cataloging-in-Publication Data is available.

ISBN 978-1-5235-2559-1

First Edition June 2025

Printed in China on responsibly sourced paper.

10 9 8 7 6 5 4 3 2 1

To my Nani, Dadi, and Mom

Contents

Preface

As an Indian American lifelong vegetarian—and part-time vegan for many years—I have amassed a lifetime of plant-based dishes that are nourishing and satisfying. Developing my home cooking habits into researched, polished recipes has brought me closer to my heritage, and taught me more about Indian culinary history than I ever imagined knowing.

My mother cooked every day for our family when I was growing up, Indian food, often with an inventive twist on it. We would try new dishes at family friends' homes or in restaurants, and she would come home and re-create them from taste alone. Her own mother, my nani (grandmother), was the same way. Whenever I visited Delhi as a child, I begged for pasta, and my grandma swiftly taught herself to make noodles from scratch—despite never seeing a recipe. My mom's and nani's creativity in the kitchen always pushed me to see what dishes I could create using the ingredients around me.

As a Northern California girl, fresh seasonal produce is the centerpiece of my life and culinary habits. When I was young, my family took trips to the Sunday morning farmers market in place of regular grocery store visits—it reminded my parents of sorting through vegetables at roadside stalls in Delhi. During my mid-college trips home for holidays, my dad and I spent hours "fruit shopping," which entails exactly what it sounds like: patiently smelling, feeling, and picking the absolute best summer stone fruit or winter squashes. Family road trips across the West Coast included regular pit stops at roadside fruit stalls, Memorial Day weekends were blocked off for family cherry picking, and visits to my great-aunt's house in the East Bay always ended in me raiding her fig tree.

When I was younger, my mom allowed my brother and me to tinker with cocktail samosas and cheese boards for her dinner parties, but she eventually brought us in for full-on menu planning. After leaving home and my mom's well-stocked fridge, I longed to fill a kitchen of my own. As I reached adulthood, my love for cooking and for fresh varieties of produce only grew. Years of playing host next to my mom trained me for what would become my current passion: hosting supper clubs in my cozy, light-filled Victorian San Francisco apartment. My first apartment was not big, but we managed to fit in an eight-person dining table, where my vegan roommates and I would host elaborate meals of ratatouille and tofu bourguignon. I still own that dining table, and all these years later it has seen hundreds of dinner parties and endless conversation.

From my loving relationship with grocery shopping to the produce-heavy diet of Indian cuisine, my life has been defined by fresh, beautiful, creative food, and my goal for this book is to share that. Along the way, conducting research for these recipes rewarded me with reminders of my past and a foreshadowing of my future. I can now replay digital voice memos from my great-aunts explaining how to make a specific mango pickle that I cannot find anywhere online. And should I ever feel bored in the kitchen, I know to reread handwritten Hindi letters from extended family, complete with a twenty-one-ingredient list to make "flavored salt"—a recipe I have still not been able to re-create. I cherish my mother's recipe-turned-poem that describes how she makes her kheer (rice pudding), with romantic visions in each step. Now this book rests in your hands, on your coffee table or shelf, and my final reward will be the memories you make with the recipes inside of it.

Between California produce, countless Hindi translations, and decades of making Indian food, this book came to life. Each recipe will equip you with straightforward skills to make plant-based Indian dishes, with both deep insight and love for the cuisine. I hope you enjoy learning to cook the way I do.

Srishti Jain

Introduction

Across all corners of India, you will find dinner tables set with rich legume stews, turmeric-coated vegetables, rice, flatbreads, and crunchy salads. Street food vendors sauce mouthwatering fritters with tangy tamarind and herb chutneys. Modern restaurants serve lentil curries simmered for upwards of twenty-four hours. Indian-Chinese fusion dishes revamp noodles and tofu with chiles and honey. Indian cuisine has no shortage of techniques to diversify the texture and taste of plant-based dishes: You can use cashews to thicken sauces, fry lentils in a batter until crisp, and adorn rice with jewel-like peas and carrots. This variety of vegetarian cuisine is unexplored by many—not to mention the range of vegan Indian dishes, which are even more untapped.

Plant-based proteins and Indian cooking have always gone hand in hand. With almost half of the nation relying on vegetable-heavy diets, vegan traditions and recipes are abundant across the country. A vast majority of Indian food culture stems from Hinduism and Jainism, two leading religious identities that prohibit animal consumption and harm to animals. This gave rise to the plant-based expertise behind Indian recipes—many of them are already inherently vegan, no substitutions needed. Because animal-free eating has existed in South Asia for so long, an array of plant-based proteins, such as lentils, tofu, and beans, are employed in dishes in myriad ways. Farming and climate conditions dictate the local cuisines across India's vast geography; the country's twenty-eight states and seemingly infinite culinary traditions leave no vegetable nor lentil unexplored. Rajasthan's dry, arid farmland lends itself to growing pulses, resulting in a variety of dishes based on besan (chickpea flour). North India relies on wheat as the primary grain, and mills fine whole wheat flour to make thin flatbreads like rotis and flaky parathas (pan-fried laminated breads). The South of India tells a different story—because of rain patterns, Southern Indians have traditionally had more access to rice. An abundance of lush paddies in

Tamil Nadu and Kerala has allowed creative uses of rice in fermented batters and steamed savory cakes to soak up sauces and curries. The wet climate encourages fragrant spices to grow and be used to intricately decorate simple recipes; dried curry leaves and mustard seeds are abundant, fried together in hot oil to perfume daals with their aroma. Even with these regional specialties, legumes, rice, and fresh vegetables remain ubiquitous across the country.

Legumes are a staple in Desi (immigrant Indian) households, whether they are used in thick, saucy curries and daals (lentil stews) or cooked dry and tossed with lemon and chutney for chaat (street food). Kidney beans, chickpeas, and peas are used whole or split in stews, and also ground into flours. Indian farmers cultivated lentils as early as 2800 BCE, and households have always cooked daal with a recipe similar to what is common today. Legumes spread as ideal crops because they do not need much water and are self-pollinating—a plant-based protein source to be eaten by many. Centuries of culinary tradition engendered infinite uses of legumes, from soups to crepes to sweet puddings. The key to mastering legumes is to make a simple curry: Go-To Lentil Curry (page 88) introduces you to cooking smaller legumes quickly, until they become creamy and absorb warm spices like turmeric, cumin, and coriander. All-Day Chickpea Curry (page 80) guides you through the magic of cooking a heartier bean like the chickpea slowly and on low heat until it becomes soft and the skin is falling off. Once you master cooking these legumes, you can start harnessing other delicious—and no less simple—forms. Chile "Cheese" Lentil Pancakes (page 17) turn ground lentils into a batter to make savory pancakes that you can eat for breakfast, lunch, or dinner. Garlic and Leek Lentil Fritters (page 39) teaches you how to make crunchy vegetable fritters coated in a lentil-based batter. Combining besan (a gluten-free flour made from ground dried chickpeas) and water instantly creates a thick batter for coating and frying any vegetable into a quick and crispy snack.

Indian recipes will teach you to treat each vegetable with distinct care. Sabzis (vegetable stir-fries) turn complicated vegetables like eggplant and okra into tender vessels of aromatics and spice. The formula of most sabzis calls for sautéing a base of alliums and spices, then coating and cooking a vegetable in it—an inherently vegan process that is the norm in Indian households. However simple sabzis may be, Indian culinary traditions know no limit to intricate vegetable recipes beyond just sautéing them in a pan. In Spinach with Whole Roasted Cauliflower (page 83), a whole cauliflower head is roasted until it is falling apart and ready to be mixed into a cooked spinach curry. Rasam Cabbage Rolls (page 71) use cabbage as a wrapper for a lentil and rice stuffing. The more you repeat stuffing, battering, and stir-frying each vegetable, the greater your understanding will be of how tender or crispy each piece of produce should be.

In addition to a rainbow of vegetables and legumes, Indian cooking equally celebrates grains that don't often show up in Western cooking but are easy to master making. Poha (flattened rice), upma (ground semolina, like Cream of Wheat), and dalia (cracked wheat) are just a few of the grains you will encounter. Savory oatmeal and saucy grits are nothing new to Indian breakfast lovers. These cereals provide a variety of textures that show how Indians have artfully created countless dishes without meat or dairy for centuries. Semolina is used in dry porridges like Braised Spring Pea–Semolina Porridge (page 33) and also in sweet, creamy puddings like kheer (page 153). Rice is one of the most common grains, and is found on the table next to daals and sabzis to provide a cooling and neutral canvas to contrast with the spices of these mains. Rice can also be used in biryani, dotted with dried fruits, nuts, and vegetables, to make it a hearty main. Atta, the fine whole wheat flour used to make rotis (thin wheat flatbreads) is yet another grain product abundant in India. Alongside rice you will find rotis, ready to scoop up vegetables and dip into curry.

Mass migrations from India to the United States starting in the 1980s led to heavy American influences on Indian dishes. California is home to the largest population of Indian immigrants in the United States. In the 1980s, it was not easy to find niche Indian vegetables in suburban US grocery stores, so Indian restaurants would make modifications to traditional dishes. Sautéing zucchini instead of bottle gourd squash into sambar (lentil stew) or wilting spinach in place of mustard greens for palak (greens curry) became the norm. Some of these vegan recipes pay homage to the melting pot of flavors born from cooking American produce with an Indian flair.

With these recipes, you'll learn to make modern but authentic plant-based South Asian dishes. Similarly, you will learn how to treat vegetables and grains in ways that you can apply universally. With each battered pakora or pickled onion you make, you are equipped with a new method for transforming your vegetables into creative Indian-inspired dishes. After the tenth time you reach for your masala dabba (spice box), you will have built an innate understanding of how to layer spices and salt within any type of dish. The more vegetables you cook with, the more familiar you will become with their different textures, and you can then feel confident substituting produce based on what is in season. Steaming perfectly fluffy rice every time becomes muscle memory. Every recipe equips you with foundational tips and tricks so you can learn the rules and then break them. As you repeat the techniques and traditions, you will be equipped to take your own liberties, too.

Indian recipes are not traditionally written—measurements are estimated and techniques are passed down orally. Eastern chefs rely on intuition, which is difficult to teach or write down, but is cultivated over years of exposure to cooking. Use this book like a musical instrument—practice the recipes, then start to make them without checking the book as often. Add your own flair using the ingredients that are most accessible to you. Taste and adjust the quantities of spices to see how the flavors of your dish change. Indian food represents centuries' worth of traditions, and with the right intentions, you will continue shaping it.

Keep Your Kitchen Stocked

An Indian pantry brims with whole and ground spices, stocks of dried legumes and pulses, and flours of all types. Keep these and other basic ingredients handy to simplify your cooking—having onions, tomatoes, garlic, and ginger around will allow you to start any main dish. Having at least one type of lentil or bean automatically sets you up for dinner. Keep your pantry full to be ready for any Indian dish you crave. See Resources, page 169, to find ingredients you can't source from a local Indian, South Asian, or regular grocery.

SPICES

SALT

Table salt's fine granules dissolve quickly and evenly into curries and on vegetables. It is especially "salty" because of how small the granules are—1 teaspoon of this salt will add more salt flavor than the same volume of the coarser grains of kosher salt. If using salt with larger grains, opt for using 1½ times the volume of table salt.

GARAM MASALA

Garam masala is the soul of Indian cooking. With its blend of cinnamon, cardamom, cloves, cumin, and coriander, this spice blend adds a warm depth to both savory and sweet dishes. Making your own garam masala (page 146) will result in the freshest and most impactful flavor.

RED CHILI POWDER

Most Indian households have their own preference for which red chili powder they like. Kashmiri red chili powder is known for its vibrant scarlet hue and mild taste, but the blend found in most Indian stores, simply labeled "red chili powder," adds a spice even greater than cayenne, so use it sparingly.

GROUND TURMERIC

The golden hue and health benefits of turmeric are what make it so popular in South Asian cuisine. It's used in grains, stews, and vegetables; turmeric blends well into most dishes. Beyond its vibrant color, this spice imparts a subtle earthiness to your recipes. A little goes a long way with turmeric and its woody, peppery taste.

GROUND CORIANDER POWDER

Coriander powder is made by grinding cilantro seeds. It offers a gentle citrusy undertone and a hint of sweetness. The versatile spice contributes a subtle herbaceous and earthy essence to dishes. Most commonly used for lentils and vegetable dishes, dried coriander powder complements the warmth of other spices like turmeric and cumin.

CUMIN

Cumin takes the form of both seeds and powder (ground) in Indian cooking. Both possess a warm, earthy flavor and a subtle peppery undertone. Seeds are used when the texture and pungent notes of cumin flavor are wanted, such as when coating roasted potatoes or grilled okra. Ground cumin imparts a more uniform flavor to sauces or curries. Most recipes using the seeds call for toasting the spice in hot oil to release its flavor.

BLACK MUSTARD SEEDS

These small, round seeds have a distinct sharpness and heat, along with a slightly bitter undertone. Dishes are often finished with a tempering of mustard seeds in hot oil to crisp them and release their aroma before adding them to bowls of simmered lentils or saucy tofu.

CARDAMOM

Cardamom is distinctly floral and is often paired with other warm and sweet spices. Whole green cardamom pods are most commonly used in Indian dishes—they have the freshest aroma and taste. These small, aromatic pods contain notes of citrus, mint, and herbal undertones that pair well with both sweet and savory dishes.

KALA NAMAK

Kala namak (black salt) is a type of rock salt known for its sulfurous, eggy scent and taste. This unique flavor profile makes it a popular ingredient in various traditional dishes, particularly in vegan and vegetarian cuisines, where it is used to mimic the flavor of eggs. It also adds a subtle smoky note to savory dishes.

AMCHOOR

Amchoor (dried mango powder) adds sourness and tang to many dishes—it mimics the flavor of lemon juice while also lending umaminess, much like a tomato. It is made from unripe (green) mangoes.

PANTRY

PULSES

The variety of pulses in South Asian pantries ranges from small red lentils to large chickpeas and lima beans. Lentils are commonly cooked to make daal (lentil stew), but also are sometimes used raw to make batter for cheelas (lentil pancakes) and piyajus (lentil fritters). Beans are cooked for hours and absorb spices well, making them common contenders for curries. (For more information, see The Daal Glossary on page 85.)

RICE

Basmati is the most popular rice used in Indian cuisine, lauded for its floral fragrance and lack of starch. When cooked, the long grains remain separate and fluffy, contributing to a light and airy texture that works well with thick and heavy curries.

CASHEWS

Besides adding a crunch to some desserts, the high fat content of cashews make them ideal to impart a creaminess to curries. Cashew cream, made from blending softened raw cashews with water, is commonly used to thicken and mellow tomato-heavy dishes. Buy whole or halved raw cashews.

SEMOLINA

Semolina, coarsely ground durum wheat, is used for breads, porridges, and fluffy puddings. Opt for whole semolina grains (sooji) rather than ground flour—the granular texture is what gives a depth to dishes like upma; it works well with nuts and fruits in kheer (page 153) and halwa (page 159).

BESAN

Besan, also known as gram flour or chickpea flour, is a versatile gluten-free flour ground from chickpeas or chana daal (split chickpeas). It is used for its distinct nutty and earthy taste. When fried, it becomes crisper than all-purpose flour, making it ideal for fritters and pancakes.

ATTA

Atta is a type of whole wheat flour made from grinding whole wheat grains, including the bran and germ, resulting in a flour that retains more nutrients compared to refined wheat flour. Atta is finer than traditional whole wheat flour, resulting in an airy texture when cooked. Its nutritional value, hearty flavor, and slight sweetness make it great for Indian flatbreads and unleavened breads like roti and paratha.

OIL

Because Indian food relies so heavily on spices to impart flavors into dishes, neutral oils such as canola, avocado, and vegetable (soybean) are used most often to create a plain base to work on top of. Olive oil also works well with vegetables that benefit from the nuttiness when roasted.

JAGGERY

Jaggery, or coconut palm sugar, has a molasses-like taste reminiscent of toffee. It can be found in the form of a block, cubes, or sometimes powder. Opt for the powder or cubes, as they are easier to measure and use.

SEV

Sev are thin, salty fried chickpea-flour noodles common in Indian snack food pantries. They can be eaten plain, and they work well as a crunchy and salty topping for salads and street food. Sev is the crunchy, savory partner to a cup of sweet chai.

FRIDGE

CILANTRO

Cilantro leaves are the most common garnish for South Asian mains. Because curries and sabzis tend to be full of warming spices, cilantro relieves them with a fresh herbaceousness that balances most dishes. Keep a bunch in your fridge to cut the spice of daals and chole.

FIRM TOFU

Tofu's spongy texture makes it the best candidate to absorb tangy marinades and rich curry bases. Tofu is a great substitute for paneer, a sturdy fresh Indian cheese often found in stews and stir-fries. Similar in texture and flavor, tofu has the ability to absorb any spices it's coated in and provide a neutral base.

TAMARIND PASTE

Sourced from tamarind fruit, this convenient paste concentrates the sweet and sour flesh into a seedless, ready-to-use ingredient for tangy chutneys and soups. An Indian grocery store often has dried or concentrated tamarind, as well as whole pods, but the paste is easiest to work with because it mixes evenly in sauces and stews.

TOMATOES

Tomatoes serve as the base for many curries, providing a sourness and umami that complement creamy lentils and a texture that easily coats porous vegetables. Roma tomatoes are commonly used for vegetable and lentil dishes, while juicy heirloom tomatoes add a fresh bite to salads and cherry tomatoes lend their sweetness to chutneys and chaat.

GINGER

The slight spice and sweetness of ginger add an unexpected kick to both savory dishes and desserts. Fresh ginger also has a cooling quality similar to mint that brings down the warming tastes of cardamom and cinnamon.

GARLIC

As in other cuisines, garlic lends its pungent aroma to Indian dishes and breaks down with tomatoes and onions to create a flavor base. This base is the foundation of all daals and curries. Peel garlic easily by slicing off the hard end and lightly smashing the cloves with the flat side of your knife. The peel should flake right off.

RED ONION

The sharpness of red onion serves as the foundation for many mains. When sautéed, the onion breaks down to add a sweet flavor needed to enhance vegetables and soup.

FRESH CHILE PEPPERS

Green chile peppers like jalapeños and Thai chiles are always on hand in an Indian kitchen to add brightness and spice. If you are worried about making your dish too spicy, deseed the chile pepper before using it.

Breakfast

Sunday breakfast in an Indian household is a five-hour affair, full of multiple courses, dishes both sweet and savory, and endless rounds of chai or coffee. Take some cues from North and South Indians alike and create a breakfast spread filled with warm, comforting porridge or sweet oatmeal, crispy lentil pancakes, and stuffed flatbreads.

Tofu Scramble

Bhurji (scramble) is a popular North Indian breakfast, traditionally made with paneer or eggs. Tofu is a hearty—and nutritious—replacement that provides a similar texture and taste. The turmeric and kala namak inject satisfying hits of umami and color into this nutritious, veggie-filled breakfast.

SERVES 4

- 1 red onion, peeled
- 2 medium Roma tomatoes
- 1 red bell pepper, stem, ribs, and seeds removed
- 3 garlic cloves, peeled
- 1-inch (2.5 cm) piece fresh ginger, peeled
- 1 fresh green chile pepper, stem removed
- 1 tablespoon vegetable oil
- 1 teaspoon cumin seeds
- 2 blocks (14 ounces/400 g each) firm tofu
- 1 teaspoon ground turmeric
- 1 teaspoon red chili powder
- 1 teaspoon kala namak (black salt)
- 2 teaspoons table salt
- ½ cup (20 g) chopped fresh cilantro, for garnish
- Toast, for serving
- Spicy Ketchup (page 139) or store-bought masala ketchup, for serving

Start by prepping the vegetables. Finely dice the onion, tomatoes, and bell pepper. Mince the garlic and ginger. Slice the green chile in half lengthwise, and keep or discard the seeds, depending on how spicy you want the bhurji. Mince the chile.

Heat a large nonstick skillet over medium heat and add the oil and cumin seeds. Fry the cumin seeds until they start crackling, about 2 minutes. Add the onion, tomatoes, bell pepper, garlic, ginger, and chile. Sauté until the onion and garlic are translucent and beginning to turn a light golden brown, about 5 minutes.

Drain the water from the tofu and pat it dry with paper towels. Using your hands, crumble the tofu into the pan, leaving some chunky 1-inch (2.5 cm) pieces. (The texture should mimic scrambled eggs.) Add the turmeric, red chili powder, kala namak, and table salt. Cook everything together for 5 to 7 minutes, until any excess water has evaporated and the tofu is slightly browned.

Sprinkle the chopped cilantro on the bhurji, then transfer to plates. Serve with toast and Spicy Ketchup.

Rose Water French Toast

SHAHI TUKDA

Shahi tukda translates literally to "a piece of royalty." True to its luxurious namesake, this dish maintains its traditional richness with the use of a fragrant rose and cardamom sugar syrup and creamy reduced oat milk. You'll get the best results with day-old bread, but if you don't want to wait, you can dry fresh bread first by baking it in a 325°F (160°C) oven for 15 minutes.

MAKES 10 PIECES TOAST; SERVES 4 TO 6

TOAST

4 tablespoons (60 g) coconut oil

10 slices dry white bread (see headnote)

ROSE SYRUP

1 tablespoon green cardamom pods

2 cups (480 ml) water

2 cups (400 g) granulated sugar

2 tablespoons rose water

CREAM

1 cup (240 ml) oat milk

½ cup (100 g) granulated sugar

½ cup (65 g) chopped pistachios, for garnish

Melt 1 tablespoon of the coconut oil in a large nonstick skillet over medium heat. Adding a few bread slices at a time, fry the bread on both sides until golden brown and crispy, about 5 minutes. Add more coconut oil, 1 tablespoon at a time, as needed. Set the fried bread slices aside while preparing the rose syrup.

Crush the cardamom pods with the flat side of a chef's knife or with a mortar and pestle. Combine the water, sugar, rose water, and crushed cardamom in a small saucepan and place over low heat. Bring to a simmer and stir, allowing the sugar to dissolve. Cook for 10 to 15 minutes, until it's thick enough to coat the back of a spoon, stirring occasionally to prevent

(continued)

burning. Pour the syrup through a fine-mesh sieve to strain out the pods and seeds into a shallow bowl. Dip each piece of bread on both sides in the syrup until the bread is fully saturated. Set aside on a large serving platter.

Heat the oat milk and sugar in a small saucepan over low heat, stirring until the sugar dissolves. Cook for 10 to 15 minutes, stirring occasionally, until the mixture has thickened like cream and can coat the back of a spoon.

Pour the cream over the fried bread, sprinkle with the pistachios, and serve.

Chile "Cheese" Lentil Pancakes

CHEELAS

Daal isn't just for Indian stews; here you use it to make crispy pancakes. Daal gets soaked, blended into a batter, pan-fried, and stuffed with shredded tofu for a hearty and complete meal. While you can use any kind of daal, or even besan (chickpea flour), in a traditional cheela using moong daal will make it healthier and easier to crisp up, too.

MAKES ABOUT 8 CHEELAS; SERVES 4

- 2 cups (400 g) moong daal (split green lentils) or masoor daal (red lentils)
- 3½ cups (840 ml) water
- 1 block (14 to 16 ounces/ 400 to 450 g) firm tofu
- 1 tablespoon nutritional yeast
- 1 teaspoon kala namak (black salt)
- 3 or 4 jalapeño or serrano chiles
- 2 teaspoons table salt
- ½ teaspoon ground coriander
- ½ teaspoon red chili powder
- 2 tablespoons olive oil
- Spicy Ketchup (page 139) or store-bought masala ketchup, for serving

Soak the moong daal in a large mixing bowl in 3 cups (720 ml) of the water for at least 4 hours and up to 8 hours.

Drain the tofu and pat dry with paper towels. Press the tofu by wrapping the block in a clean kitchen towel and placing it on a plate or rimmed baking sheet. Put a heavy object such as a cast-iron skillet on top of it and let drain for 30 to 45 minutes.

Once the tofu is pressed and dry, use a box grater to grate it into large pieces into a separate large bowl. Combine the grated tofu with the nutritional yeast and kala namak. Slice the chiles into thin rounds and stir them into the tofu mixture.

(continued)

Drain the soaked daal and put them in a blender with the table salt, coriander, chili powder, and the remaining ½ cup (120 ml) water. Blend until it reaches a thick and smooth consistency.

Set a nonstick skillet over medium heat and add 1 tablespoon of the olive oil. Drop a bit of batter into the oil to check if it is hot enough—when the batter sizzles, it's ready. Using a ½-cup (120 ml) measure, ladle and spread the batter in the pan and sprinkle a small handful of the tofu mixture on top of the cheela. Allow the bottom and edges of the cheela to fry until brown and crispy, like you would a pancake. Flip the cheela after 3 to 4 minutes. Fry the second side of the cheela until it's golden brown and the tofu is browned slightly, another 3 minutes. Flip the cheela once more so the tofu is on top, and fold the cheela in half like a quesadilla. Transfer the cheela to a platter and cover with a kitchen towel to keep warm.

Repeat until you have used up all the batter and filling. Serve the cheelas with Spicy Ketchup.

NOTE: *The batter can be made in advance and stored in the fridge for 2 days.*

Freestyle It

- Cheelas can be made with a variety of daals, depending on what you have readily available to you. Feel free to replace the moong daal with any red or yellow daal, or even a combination of varieties. If using besan (chickpea flour), skip the soaking and grinding. Instead, combine 2 cups (180 g) flour with 1 cup (240 ml) water, the table salt, coriander, and red chili powder, and whisk to make a thick batter.

Crispy Potato Rice Flakes

POHA

The fluffiest rice dish you've ever had still won't compare to the light airiness of a bowl of poha (flattened rice). Rice is parboiled, then smashed and dried to make poha flakes, which need little cooking to soften. Seasoning and steaming poha creates a soft and fluffy dish that can take on aromas and spices just like a pilaf.

SERVES 4

- **2 medium russet potatoes (about 6 ounces/170 g each)**
- **3 teaspoons olive oil**
- **2 teaspoons table salt**
- **1 shallot, peeled**
- **1 cup (135 g) frozen green peas**
- **1 teaspoon ground turmeric**
- **1 teaspoon red chili powder**
- **2 cups (280 g) poha (rice flakes)**
- **Roasted peanuts, for garnish**
- **1 lemon, cut into wedges, for serving**
- **Spicy Ketchup (page 139) or store-bought masala ketchup, for serving**
- **Green Chutney (page 134), for serving**

Preheat the oven to 425°F (220°C). Line a baking sheet with parchment paper.

Peel the potatoes and dice them into ¼-inch (6 mm) pieces. Spread the potatoes out on the lined baking sheet. Drizzle with 2 teaspoons of the olive oil and sprinkle with 1 teaspoon of the salt; toss to combine. Roast the potatoes for 20 minutes, flipping them with a spatula at the 10-minute mark. Cook until the potatoes are a deep golden brown.

While the potatoes are roasting, finely mince the shallot. Set a Dutch oven or heavy-bottomed wide skillet over medium heat. Add the shallot to the skillet with the remaining teaspoon of oil. Rinse the frozen peas in a fine-mesh sieve under cold water to thaw them, then add them to the shallot.

(continued)

Allow the shallot and peas to soften for 5 to 6 minutes, until the peas are fully cooked. Add the turmeric, the remaining 1 teaspoon salt, and the red chili powder to the peas and shallot.

Put the poha flakes in a fine-mesh sieve. Working quickly, rinse the poha under cold water for 10 seconds, then drain and immediately add them to the skillet. (The goal is to wet the poha flakes without getting them soggy or letting them clump together.) Mix the poha with the shallot, peas, and ¼ cup (60 ml) of water and cover with a lid. Let the poha steam for 8 to 10 minutes. The poha should fluff up to a texture similar to cooked rice. Use a spoon to mix and loosen everything.

When the potatoes are golden brown and crispy, remove them from the oven. Plate the poha in shallow bowls, then top with a handful of the potatoes and a spoonful of roasted peanuts. Squeeze the lemon over everything. Serve with Spicy Ketchup and Green Chutney.

Flaky Butternut Squash Flatbread

PARATHA

Parathas are buttery laminated flatbreads and one of the most common Indian breakfasts that you will find. They can be eaten any which way you desire—plain, with yogurt and Pickled Onions (page 130), or stuffed with any spiced vegetable in season. Butternut squash adds an autumnal spin to the common paratha, which is traditionally vegan and relies on oil to create rich, flaky layers.

MAKES 8 PARATHAS; SERVES 4 TO 6

1 small butternut squash (about 8 ounces/220 g)

4 tablespoons (60 ml) vegetable oil, plus more for greasing and spreading

3 teaspoons table salt

2 batches Whole Wheat Flatbread dough (page 110), prepared through kneading

½ red onion, peeled

3 garlic cloves, peeled

2 teaspoons ground cumin

1 teaspoon red chili powder

½ cup (20 g) chopped fresh cilantro

Atta for rolling

Pickled Onions (page 130) or Pickled Ginger and Chiles (page 131), for serving

Preheat the oven to 425°F (220°C). Line a baking sheet with parchment paper.

Cut the butternut squash in half lengthwise and use a spoon to scoop out and discard the seeds. Rub the squash halves with 1 tablespoon of the oil and sprinkle 1 teaspoon of the salt on the interior flesh. Place both halves, cut side down, on the lined baking sheet and pierce each half a few times with a fork. Bake for 40 minutes, or until the inside of the squash is tender. Allow the squash to cool before scooping out the flesh into a mixing bowl. Discard the peels.

While the squash is in the oven, rest the dough for 30 minutes.

(continued)

Mince the onion and garlic. Add them to the squash along with cumin, the remaining 2 teaspoons salt, red chili powder, and cilantro. Use a fork or potato masher to combine the ingredients thoroughly, until smooth.

Divide the dough into 8 equal portions. Lightly coat your hands with oil and roll each portion between your palms to form a ball about the size of a golf ball. Lay a clean kitchen towel over the balls to prevent them from drying out.

To assemble the parathas, start by flouring a clean countertop. Using a rolling pin, roll out a dough ball into a circle about 4 inches (10 cm) in diameter. Scoop 3 tablespoons of the squash mixture onto the middle of the dough, and bring up the edges of the dough together, tightly pinching the dough into a ball. Repeat with the remaining dough balls and squash filling.

Gently roll out each filled dough ball with the rolling pin, this time to a circle 6 inches (15 cm) in diameter. Be careful to not apply too much pressure while rolling, so you don't squeeze out the filling. Spread a few drops of oil across the surface of the circle with your fingers or a pastry brush; the circle should be fully coated with oil. Roll the circle into a long cylinder then coil the dough to create a spiral shape. You should end up with a tight spiral, similar to a snail shell shape. With the rolling pin, roll out each paratha a third and final time into a circle, about 6 inches (15 cm) in diameter.

Let the parathas rest under a clean kitchen towel while you heat a cast-iron skillet or tawa over medium-high heat. Drizzle 1½ teaspoons oil into the pan and swirl it around to evenly spread it across the base. When the pan is hot and the oil is shiny, place a paratha in the pan. Cook for 4 to 5 minutes, until the bottom is golden brown. Use a spatula to move it around from time to time to ensure it's not sticking to the pan. Flip the paratha and cook for another 4 to 5 minutes on the other side, until it's deeply golden brown. Wrap the cooked paratha in a clean kitchen towel to keep warm while you cook the remaining parathas, making sure to re-oil the pan before placing the next one down. Serve warm, with the pickle(s) of your choice.

Freestyle It

- If you don't have butternut squash, any starchy root vegetable in the same quantity, like potatoes, yams, or taro, can take its place.

Spiced Potato Sandwiches with Jalapeño Chutney

Potatoes in a sandwich may seem like a surprising filling, but their fluffy texture and heartiness make them a hit on menus in Indian canteens, as well as a favorite of many North Indian children. Potato sandwiches are commonly served with spicy ketchup or full of green chiles, but a sweet and spicy jalapeño chutney binds together this breakfast favorite. Use the chutney with other dishes, such as for dipping Chile "Cheese" Lentil Pancakes (page 17) or topping Crispy Potato Rice Flakes (page 21).

MAKES 8 SANDWICHES; SERVES 4 TO 6

JALAPEÑO CHUTNEY

10 jalapeño chiles, stems removed (about 14 ounces/400 g total)

2 cups (400 g) granulated sugar

1 cup (240 ml) water

1 teaspoon table salt

SANDWICHES

4 russet potatoes (about 6 ounces/170 g each), scrubbed

4 teaspoons table salt

1 teaspoon amchoor (dried mango powder)

1 teaspoon ground coriander

1 red onion, peeled

¼ cup (10 g) chopped fresh cilantro

16 slices bread of your choice

2 tablespoons (30 g) plant-based butter

Mince the jalapeños. Combine the jalapeños, sugar, water, and salt in a medium heavy-bottomed saucepan and set it over medium-low heat. Stir constantly while the mixture begins to simmer. The jalapeños should be coated in the sugar and start to get sticky. Cook the chutney for 10 to 15 minutes, until it has a jam-like consistency. If the mixture begins to tighten up, making it difficult to stir, add a few splashes of water. Once the chutney is no longer runny, remove the saucepan from the heat and allow it to cool.

(continued)

Put potatoes in a large pot and fill it with water at least 2 inches (5 cm) above the potatoes. Add 2 teaspoons of the salt and bring to a boil over medium heat. Cook the potatoes for about 20 minutes, until fork-tender.

Drain the potatoes in a colander and run them under cold water to cool them. Peel the potatoes, cut them into large chunks, and add them to a large mixing bowl. Sprinkle with the amchoor, coriander, and the remaining 2 teaspoons salt. Mince the onion and add it and the cilantro to the potatoes. Using a fork, your hands, or a potato masher, mash the potatoes and thoroughly combine them with the spices and herbs.

Set a cast-iron skillet or tawa over medium heat.

To make each sandwich, coat one side of a slice of bread with jalapeño chutney, and spread a few heaping spoons of the potato mixture on a second slice. Press the two together to form a sandwich. Spread a small pat of butter on the exterior of both sides of the sandwich. Place the sandwich on the hot pan and gently press down on it with a spatula. Cook for 4 to 5 minutes on one side, until the bread is light golden brown and toasted. Flip the sandwich and press down again—you are trying to give the sandwich a panini-like density and texture. Once the sandwich is cooked, it should be toasted on both sides and sealed shut. Repeat with the remaining bread, chutney, and potato mixture. Serve the sandwiches while still hot, cut diagonally into two triangles.

Freestyle It

› If you don't have potatoes on hand or don't have the time to boil them, get creative! You can use 3 cups of frozen tots or hash browns instead. Cook them according to their package instructions, then place some on top of the jalapeño chutney before closing the sandwiches with the second slice of bread. Butter and toast the sandwiches as directed.

Equipping Your Tool Chest

A stocked Indian kitchen includes special tools for cooking vegetables until they are exceptionally tender and rolling out the thinnest flatbreads. The necessary trifecta of gadgets comprises a masala dabba (spice box), belan (rolling pin), and tawa (cast-iron pan).

Masala dabbas house the most-reached-for whole and ground spices in an Indian kitchen. Each katori (steel bowl) arranged inside the large, round dabba contains basic spices such as salt, turmeric, and red chili powder. Masala dabbas come with a tight-fitting lid—keep it on when you are not using the spices to prevent them from losing their aroma. A small teaspoon accompanies each katori to make spice measuring and adding easy. It is important that each bowl has its own spoon to prevent cross-contamination and keep the spices pure. Beyond the basic spices, dabbas diverge based on region and personal preference. Mustard seeds, whose bitterness complements the coconut shreds often present in South Indian cooking, are found in Tamilian and Keralan masala boxes. North Indians use cumin and coriander seeds more liberally, making those whole spices mainstays in Punjabi dabbas. Stock your kitchen's masala dabba with the spices you cook with most often, even if they are not traditionally South Asian. Review your dabba every few months to see which spices you are not touching, and replace them with something different.

Once you have set up your masala dabba to spice vegetable stir-fries and curries, you need a belan to roll out the accompanying flatbreads. Belans are traditional Indian rolling pins made of wood; unlike French rolling pins, they do not taper at the ends but instead are an even cylinder all the way through. This uniform cylinder ensures an even thickness when you roll out bread dough to a thin circle. Two narrower handles protrude from either end to make gripping the belan easy. Heavier wood is an ideal material because its weight adds stability and minimizes slippage when rolling out rotis (whole wheat flatbreads). The treated material of a belan also minimizes sticking, leaving the uncooked dough pristine and matte while it is rolled out.

After you roll rotis into rounds, they are transferred to a tawa to cook. A tawa is a shallow, concave frying pan made from cast iron or aluminum. The circular shape of the pan mimics the circles that parathas and other unleavened breads are rolled into. It functions similarly to a cast-iron skillet—it's able to conduct heat, making the tawa the ideal tool for cooking dough quickly into airy, puffed naan and roti flatbreads. Its nonstick quality also makes a tawa a desirable cooking vessel: Tawas only require the basic seasoning of rubbing them down with oil from time to time; as long as you do not cook wet foods on them, they will maintain their sheen and texture. Mastering a tawa takes trial and error—the first time you lay a rolled roti onto one, it may not puff up or cook evenly. To troubleshoot this, test if your tawa is hot enough before using it by dropping a sprinkle of water directly onto the pan. If the water immediately sizzles and steams, the tawa is ready for cooking the flatbread.

Equip yourself with these tools to create impressive Indian meals. If anything, outfitting your kitchen with this new cookware will motivate you to take on another recipe and improve your cooking across all cuisines.

Cracked Wheat with Poached Rhubarb

DALIA

Dalia, also known as cracked wheat or broken wheat, can be used to make a sweet or savory porridge for breakfast. The sweet version is not too cloying, and is reminiscent of a milkier oatmeal. Rhubarb provides sourness to the rich porridge, while warming spices like cloves and jaggery give the breakfast an unexpected depth. Jaggery tastes nutty and like molasses, resembling the caramelized flavors of sugarcane and dates.

SERVES 4

4 cups (1 L) water

4 rhubarb stalks (about 12 ounces/350 g total)

1 cup (190 g) jaggery

2 tablespoons whole cloves

1 tablespoon (15 g) plant-based butter

2 cups (230 g) dalia (cracked wheat)

4 cups (1 L) plant-based milk of your choice

¼ cup (50 g) granulated sugar

Pinch of table salt

2 tablespoons roasted pistachios, roughly chopped

Bring the water to a boil in a large pot. Slice off both ends from the rhubarb stalks, then cut each stalk into 3-inch (8 cm) pieces. Once the water is boiling, add the rhubarb, jaggery, and cloves. Lower the heat to medium-low and allow the rhubarb to poach for about 6 minutes; it should be fork-tender when ready, but not falling apart.

Melt the butter in a heavy-bottomed saucepan or Dutch oven over medium-low heat. Add the dalia and stir to coat it, lightly toasting it for 4 to 5 minutes, until lightly browned. Lower the heat and stir in the milk, granulated sugar, and salt.

(continued)

Allow the milk to reach a hard simmer, when there are small, rapid bubbles surfacing, then reduce the heat to low. Cook the dalia for 12 to 14 minutes. The goal is to cook the dalia to at least al dente, but you can cook it to whatever softness you desire. Stir the porridge often to prevent the milk from burning and the grains from sticking to the bottom of the pan.

Divide the cooked porridge into four bowls. Using tongs or a spider, remove the rhubarb from the poaching liquid and divide it among the bowls; spoon the juice on top of each bowl of dalia. Sprinkle chopped pistachios on each bowl.

Store extra dalia in an airtight container in the fridge for up to 4 days. Dalia can also be enjoyed cold.

Freestyle It

- If rhubarb is out of season, dalia can be topped with any other poached fruit. Try it with peaches, pears, or quince, depending on the season. Add diced peaches to the poaching liquid and poach for 7 minutes. If using apples, quince, or pears, peel, halve, and core them and follow the same poaching instructions, but make sure to poach for at least 12 minutes or until they're to your desired softness.

Braised Spring Pea–Semolina Porridge

UPMA

This thick and comforting upma (semolina porridge) pairs with sweet spring peas for a breakfast that redefines oatmeal. Braising spring peas with lemon juice adds sweetness and sourness to the dish that complement the rich and buttery mouthfeel of the upma. Upma started as a South Indian staple and is now pervasive through many Indian and Indian American households. Adding cashews, uncooked chana daal, and curry leaves gives the porridge an extra crunch.

SERVES 4

UPMA

1 tablespoon olive oil

2 cups (360 g) semolina (ground durum wheat, like Cream of Wheat)

1 shallot, peeled

1 fresh green chile pepper, stem removed

¼ cup (30 g) raw cashews

1 tablespoon chana daal (split chickpeas)

1 teaspoon black mustard seeds

1 teaspoon cumin seeds

4 cups (1 L) water

2 teaspoons table salt

BRAISED SPRING PEAS

4 garlic cloves, peeled

2 cups (290 g) shelled spring peas (see Freestyle It)

Juice of 1 lemon

1 teaspoon ground cumin

1 teaspoon ground coriander

1 teaspoon table salt

¼ cup (60 ml) water

Set a heavy-bottomed saucepan over medium heat. Pour in the olive oil. Add the semolina and toss to coat it evenly in the oil. Continually stir and toast the grains until they are light golden brown, 5 to 6 minutes.

(continued)

Finely mince the shallot and green chile. Add to the toasted semolina along with the cashews, chana daal, mustard seeds, and cumin seeds. Cook for 4 to 5 minutes, until the spices are fragrant and the shallot is browning. Stir in the water and salt. Bring to a boil, then reduce the heat to low. Cover the pot and cook for 4 to 5 minutes, until the water has been absorbed, the semolina looks fluffed up, and its granules appear larger. Use a fork or spoon to loosen the upma, then remove it from the heat. Keep it covered while making the peas.

Slice the garlic crosswise into thin chips. Combine the peas, garlic, lemon juice, ground cumin, coriander, salt, and water in a nonstick or cast-iron skillet and place over medium-low heat. Simmer until the peas are soft and starting to burst, 5 to 6 minutes.

Divide the upma into individual bowls, top with the peas, and serve.

Freestyle It:

- The same quantity of frozen peas can be used in place of fresh peas; just rinse them with water to thaw before cooking. Lima beans or drained canned chickpeas would also taste great, either in addition to or in place of the peas. Make sure to season accordingly and add more lemon juice if using bigger beans.

Chai & Chaat

Chai is more than just milky black tea—it's a lifestyle. Chai is also the afternoon meal of salty snacks that come with it, the gossip as you fry up some crunchy pakoras (fritters), and the act of cutting apples for fruit chaat (fruit salad) with your family. Chaat is the collective name for these salty snacks that you can often inhale in one bite while drinking your tea.

Oat Milk Chai

Every Indian caffeine addict probably has their own method of making chai. Chai recipes vary in their water-to-milk ratio, ginger grating technique, and the concoction of warm spices. This version uses oat milk to lend the chai a velvety mouthfeel that no other milk can match, as well as a combination of fresh ginger and cardamom that adds an aromatic kick to complement the richness of the chai.

SERVES 4

3 cups (720 ml) water
1 cup (240 ml) oat milk
4 black tea bags
3 tablespoons granulated sugar
2-inch (5 cm) piece fresh ginger, peeled
1 star anise pod
1 teaspoon whole cloves
1 teaspoon green cardamom pods

Combine the water, oat milk, tea bags, and sugar in a medium saucepan and set it over low heat. Place the ginger, star anise, cloves, and cardamom in a mortar or small, sturdy bowl. Using a pestle or muddler, smash the ginger and spices together a few times until the ginger and cardamom are cracked open. The ginger should be fragrant.

Add the crushed ginger and spices to the chai and stir a few times to make sure the sugar is fully dissolved. Allow the chai to slowly come to a boil; keeping the heat on low will allow the spices time to fully steep and flavor the chai. The chai should simmer for at least 5 minutes, but can go for up to 30 minutes to enhance its flavor. Keep an eye on the chai to prevent it from boiling over. Once the chai hits a boil and is deep golden brown in color, turn off the heat.

One at a time, set a small fine-mesh sieve over four mugs and strain the chai into each. Serve the chai while still piping hot.

Garlic and Leek Lentil Fritters

PIYAJUS

Piyajus, or red lentil fritters, do not rely on any wheat or rice flour to guarantee their crunchy magic. Instead, soaked raw red lentils get blended directly into the spiced fritter batter. The lentils transform into a crunchy fritter unmatched by any other batter, and lend an unexpected nuttiness to every bite. Thinly sliced garlic and leeks pair well with the inherent buttery flavor of lentils, while the bits of leek poking out of the piyajus get delightfully frizzled.

MAKES 14 TO 16 PIYAJUS

1 cup (200 g) masoor daal (red lentils)

2 cups (480 ml) water

5 teaspoons kosher salt

½ teaspoon ground cumin

½ teaspoon red chili powder

5 garlic cloves, peeled

2 leeks (about 3 ounces/90 g each), root ends trimmed, white and light green parts only

4 cups (1 L) vegetable oil

Spicy Ketchup (page 139) or store-bought masala ketchup, for serving

Combine the masoor daal and water in a large bowl. Loosely cover the bowl with a kitchen towel. Soak for at least 4 hours or up to 12 hours.

Drain the masoor daal in a large fine-mesh sieve. Add them to a blender or food processor along with 1 teaspoon of the salt, ½ cup (240 ml) of water, the cumin, and red chili powder. Blend until a thick paste forms, about 2 minutes. Check the batter's consistency, making sure some small pieces of lentils remain to make the fritter as crispy as possible.

Slice the garlic crosswise into thin chips. Slice the leeks into coins about ⅛-inch (3 mm) thick. Rinse the leeks thoroughly in a colander under cold water; drain well.

(continued)

Transfer the batter into a large mixing bowl, making sure to scrape the sides of the blender with a spatula to remove all the bits of batter. Add the garlic and leeks and use a large spoon or your hands to combine the batter with the alliums to ensure they are thoroughly coated.

Set up a frying station: Pour the oil into a large, heavy-bottomed pot (a Dutch oven, cast-iron pot, or wok works well), and set it over medium-high heat. Line a plate with paper towels and set it nearby. Place the remaining 4 teaspoons salt in a bowl you can access easily.

Heat the oil for 10 to 15 minutes, until it reaches 350°F (175°C). If you don't have a deep-frying thermometer, check if the oil is hot enough by dropping a small bit of the batter into the oil. If it immediately rises to the surface and starts to crackle and solidify, the oil is ready.

Using a tablespoon, scoop up the batter and gently dollop it into the oil. Repeat this four or five times, but do not crowd the pot. There should be enough room to move the piyajus around to ensure they are not sticking together.

Fry the piyajus for 2 minutes on one side, until they are deeply browned, before using a spider or slotted spoon to flip them over. Fry for 2 to 3 more minutes on the other side. The piyajus should be deep tan. Use the spider to transfer the fritters to the paper towel–lined plate. Immediately sprinkle salt on them while hot to make sure the salt adheres. Piyajus can be kept hot and crispy in a 350°F (175°C) oven while you cook the rest.

Fry the remaining batter in batches. Serve the piyajus hot with Spicy Ketchup.

Store any leftover fritters in an airtight container in the refrigerator for up to 5 days. Cold piyajus can be reheated in the oven for 15 minutes at 350°F (175°C).

Freestyle It

- Though piyajus are traditionally made with red lentils, feel free to experiment with any lentil of your choice. Moong daal will also create a crispy exterior. Lentils with skins on add even more protein and nutrients to this fried treat.

Pakora Anything and Everything

Everyone loves a crunchy appetizer. And Indians are no stranger to that love. We fry battered onions, spinach, and chile peppers in a variety of flours into a golden rainbow of pakoras to serve alongside hot cups of chai and bright chutneys.

Once you have your frying technique down, you can pakora anything—run wild with what you decide to make. Use the Beet, Onion, and Shishito Fritters (page 45) for the batter base and frying method. From there, let your creative juices flow and think outside the box with the add-ins. Try your pakoras with shredded potatoes, carrots, or even fruit like blood oranges.

Stick to 1-inch-long (2.5 cm) pieces or smaller, no matter what mix-ins you choose. Every vegetable acts differently in a pakora batter, depending on its starchiness and moisture content. Hard, starchy choices like potatoes and taro should be shredded to ensure they will be cooked through entirely when fried. When working with vegetables with a lot of moisture, like zucchini or eggplant, shred or slice them and sprinkle with salt about 30 minutes before you're ready to pakora. Let them sit in a colander and release their moisture, then use paper towels to dab off any water they may have produced before adding them to the pakora batter. Produce that is mostly moisture, like tomatoes and lettuce, will become too soggy and won't get crispy, making them poor contenders for pakora. But corn and peas are already bite-sized bits that do not need any advance prep.

It's the besan (chickpea flour) that makes pakoras as delicious as they are. Its low moisture content and lack of gluten makes for more crispy, less cakey fritters than if they were made with an all-purpose flour. Besan also possesses unique binding properties when moistened, allowing the batter to cling to most vegetables. My favorite besans come from Indian grocers (see Resources, page 169)—brands like Laxmi and Deep are no-frills, good quality, and cheap. But any chickpea flour you can get your hands on will work. If you don't have chickpea flour, feel free to try a lentil batter like the one in Garlic and Leek Lentil Fritters (page 39).

Using the same batter recipe and frying instructions on page 45, swap out the beet, onion, and shishitos for one of these combinations:

GARLIC AND SHREDDED ZUCCHINI

Slice 3 garlic cloves into thin chips. Use the large holes of a box grater to shred 2 cups (500 ml) zucchini from about 4 large zucchinis. Place the zucchini shreds in a colander in the sink, sprinkle with 1 teaspoon table salt, and let sit for about 30 minutes. Wrap the shreds in a clean kitchen towel and squeeze out all the moisture. Stir the zucchini and garlic into the pakora batter and fry.

POTATO-STUFFED JALAPEÑOS

Slice a lengthwise slit in each of 12 jalapeño chiles and seed them. Make half the potato filling from Potato Sandwiches with Jalapeño Chutney (page 25) and stuff each pepper with 1 tablespoon of the potato mixture, coat in the pakora batter, and fry.

CORN, SERRANO CHILE, AND CILANTRO

For Southwestern-style pakoras, add 2 cups (500 g) fresh or frozen corn kernels, 2 tablespoons minced serrano chile, and 1 cup (40 g) chopped fresh cilantro to the batter.

APPLE AND SHREDDED POTATO, LATKE-STYLE

Shred 1 large russet potato (about 6 ounces/170 g) on the large holes of a box grater. Cut 2 apples into thin matchsticks. Stir the potato and apples into the batter and fry.

Beet, Onion, and Shishito Fritters

PAKORAS

Chai pakora—which literally means "tea fritter"—is a savory snack to devour alongside your steamiest cup of chai. Onions are a classic pakora filling, adding a crunch and subtle sweetness to the nutty chickpea batter. Beets dye these pakoras a stunning pink hue while imparting each fritter with an earthy bite.

MAKES 14 TO 16 PAKORAS

1 beet, trimmed and peeled (about 5 ounces/135 g)

1 medium red or white onion, peeled

1 cup (150 g) shishito peppers, stems removed

1 cup (90 g) besan (chickpea flour)

¼ cup (60 ml) water

5 teaspoons kosher salt

½ teaspoon ground turmeric

½ teaspoon red chili powder

4 cups (1 L) vegetable oil

Red Chutney (page 136), for serving

Green Chutney (page 134), for serving

Grate the beet on the large holes of a box grater over a cutting board, then gather the beet shreds and squeeze out any excess water with your hands into the sink. (You might want to wear gloves for this.) Place the beets in a large mixing bowl.

Cut the onion in half lengthwise. Slice the halves into thin half-moons and add to the beet. Cut the shishito peppers into ½-inch (1 cm) pieces. Add to the beet and onions.

Combine the besan, water, 2 teaspoons of the salt, the turmeric, and red chili powder in a separate large bowl. Vigorously mix the batter with a spoon until no lumps remain. The texture of the batter should not be too thin or runny; it should resemble pancake batter. If the batter is too runny,

(continued)

add more besan 1 tablespoon at a time. Add the prepared vegetables to the batter and, using a spoon or your hands, thoroughly mix the vegetables into the batter so that the vegetables are evenly coated.

Set up a frying station: Pour the oil into a large, heavy-bottomed pot (a Dutch oven, cast-iron pot, or wok will work well), and set it over medium-high heat. Line a plate with paper towels and set it nearby. Place the remaining 3 teaspoons salt in a small bowl you can access easily.

Heat the oil for 10 to 15 minutes, until it reaches 350°F (175°C). To check if the oil is hot enough, drop a small piece of the batter into the pot—if it immediately rises and starts to crackle and fry, the oil is ready. You can also use a deep-frying thermometer to check the temperature.

Using a tablespoon, scoop up the batter and dollop it into the oil. Repeat this four or five times, but do not crowd the pot. Move the pakoras around with a spider or slotted spoon to ensure they do not stick together.

Fry the pakoras for 2 to 3 minutes, until deep golden brown on one side, before using the spider to flip them over. Cook for 2 to 3 minutes on the second side, until golden brown. Use the spider to transfer the pakoras to the paper towel–lined plate. Immediately sprinkle salt on them, as the salt will stick best while the pakoras are still hot. Pakoras can be kept hot and crispy in a 350°F (175°C) oven while you cook the rest.

Fry the remaining batter in batches. Serve the pakoras hot with Red and Green Chutneys.

Cold pakoras can be reheated in the oven for 15 minutes at 350°F (175°C).

Tofu Tikki Burgers

McDonald's might be the last place you'd think to visit for a quick plant-based meal, but in India the story is different. There, McDonald's is a vegan's paradise, complete with potato patty burgers, tofu cutlets, and a range of spicy sauces to drench them all in. In this play on a masala Big Mac, tofu's spongy texture soaks up the garam masala, chaat masala, and red chili powder to ensure complexity in every bite.

SERVES 4

- 1 block (14 to 16 ounces/ 400 to 450 g) firm tofu
- 2 tablespoons olive oil
- 5 teaspoons table salt
- 2 teaspoons red chili powder
- 1 teaspoon Garam Masala (page 146, or store-bought)
- 1 teaspoon chaat masala
- 1 cup (125 g) all-purpose flour
- 1 cup (240 ml) almond or soy milk
- 2 cups (120 g) panko breadcrumbs
- 1 teaspoon ground coriander
- 2 cups (480 ml) vegetable oil
- 1 red onion, peeled
- 1 or 2 large Roma tomatoes
- ¼ cup (60 g) vegan mayonnaise
- ¼ cup (60 g) Spicy Ketchup (page 139) or store-bought masala ketchup
- 4 vegan burger buns

Drain the water from the tofu. Slice the tofu into four 30× 2-inch (8 × 5 cm) planks. Each slice should be about ½-inch (1 cm) thick. Pat dry with paper towels.

Combine the olive oil, 2 teaspoons of the salt, 1 teaspoon of the red chili powder, the garam masala, and chaat masala in a small bowl. Transfer the marinade and the slices of tofu to a large resealable bag. Shaking the bag gently, fully coat the tofu pieces with the marinade. Allow the tofu to marinate for at least 30 minutes at room temperature, or up to 4 hours in the fridge.

Using three wide, shallow bowls or 13 × 9-inch (33 × 23 cm) rimmed baking sheets, set up a dredging station. In the first bowl, put the flour; in the second bowl, the milk; and in the third bowl, mix the breadcrumbs, the remaining 1 teaspoon red chili powder, and the coriander thoroughly.

(continued)

Set up a frying station: Pour the vegetable oil into a heavy-bottomed skillet (a cast-iron skillet works well), and set it over medium-high heat. Place a wire rack over a baking sheet and keep it ready on the side, as well as a small bowl with the remaining 3 teaspoons salt.

Heat the oil for 8 to 10 minutes, until it reaches 350°F (175°C). If you don't have a deep-frying thermometer to check if the oil is hot enough, drop a small piece of the tofu into the pan. If the tofu immediately rises and sizzles, the oil is ready.

Handling 1 tofu plank at a time, toss it in the flour to cover, then shake off any excess. Transfer the plank to the bowl of milk, coat it thoroughly, and shake off any excess milk. Finally, place the tofu in the breadcrumbs, toss it lightly, and gently pat the breadcrumbs onto the tofu until it is fully coated. Set the tofu plank aside on a plate and coat another plank in the same way.

Carefully add the 2 tofu planks to the oil and fry for 2 to 3 minutes on one side. Once the underside is golden brown, use a spatula to flip the tofu over and fry on the second side for another 1 to 2 minutes, until completely golden brown on both sides. Transfer the tofu tikki burgers to the wire rack and immediately sprinkle them with salt. Repeat dredging and frying the remaining tofu planks.

Prep the burger toppings: Slice the onion into ¼-inch-thick (6 mm) rounds; slice the tomato into ½-inch-thick (1 cm) rounds. Combine the mayonnaise and ketchup in a small bowl and stir until the sauce is completely homogenous. Slice the burger buns in half and spread the sauce on both of the cut sides. Place 1 tomato slice and 1 onion slice on the bottom bun and top with a piece of tofu. Finish with the bun top and serve.

The cooked tofu patties can be frozen for up to 3 months, tightly wrapped. To reheat, place a patty in a lightly oiled nonstick skillet and cook on each side for 5 to 7 minutes.

Caramelized Onion and Potato Patties

These turnovers are reminiscent of a potato "patty" you find in Indian cafes, stuffed with delicious samosa filling. Using store-bought puff pastry allows you to skip the labor of making samosa dough and frying the pastries. The layers of puff pastry blanket the soft potato filling and sweet caramelized onions in a flaky yet tender crust. It takes some time to render the onions jammy and sweet, but the rest of the dish can be made while the onions are cooking—just remember to stir them every so often.

MAKES 8 SAMOSAS

CARAMELIZED ONIONS

2 yellow or white onions (about 10 ounces/280 g total), peeled

2 tablespoons (30 g) plant-based butter

2 tablespoons granulated sugar

2 tablespoons water

1 teaspoon table salt

SAMOSAS

3 russet potatoes (about 15 ounces/420 g total), scrubbed

2 teaspoons table salt

1 jalapeño chile, stem removed

1-inch (2.5 cm) piece fresh ginger, peeled

3 garlic cloves, peeled

1 tablespoon vegetable oil, plus more for greasing

½ cup (70 g) frozen or fresh green peas

1 teaspoon cumin seeds

1 teaspoon Garam Masala (page 146, or store-bought)

1 teaspoon red chili powder

1 box (17 ounces/490 g) vegan puff pastry (Pepperidge Farm works well)

2 tablespoons (30 g) plant-based butter

Red Chutney (page 136), for serving

Green Chutney (page 134), for serving

(continued)

Slice the onions in half lengthwise, then cut them into slices about ¼-inch (6 mm) wide. Heat a large nonstick, cast-iron, or stainless-steel skillet over medium-low heat and add the butter. After the butter melts, add the onions, sugar, water, and 1 teaspoon salt. Stir the onions every 3 minutes to prevent them from sticking or burning in the pan. After their volume has reduced by about half, reduce the heat to low. The onions will need 30 to 40 minutes to fully caramelize, until they are translucent and dark brown, with a thick, jam-like texture. Stir the onions every few minutes to ensure even cooking and promote evaporation. Once caramelized, remove the pan from the heat.

Prepare the samosa filling while the onions are caramelizing. Put the potatoes in a large pot and fill it with enough water to cover them by about 2 inches (5 cm). Add 2 teaspoons salt. Cover the pot, bring the water to a boil over medium heat, and cook the potatoes for 20 minutes or until they can be pierced all the way through with a fork.

Once the potatoes are cooked, drain them and run them under cold water to cool. Peel the potatoes with your fingers, discarding the peels. Transfer the potatoes to a large mixing bowl and mash them with a fork until they are mostly crumbled, with a few pea-sized chunks remaining.

Slit the jalapeño lengthwise and remove the seeds. Mince the jalapeño, ginger, and garlic into equally small pieces. Heat a large nonstick skillet over medium heat and add the jalapeño, ginger, garlic, and vegetable oil. Cook for 1 to 2 minutes, until fragrant and the onions start to become translucent. Stir in the peas, cumin seeds, garam masala, and red chili powder; everything should be well combined. Cook for 3 to 4 minutes, until the peas are soft and easy to mush. Add the mashed potatoes and mix to thoroughly combine.

Transfer the filling to a large, shallow bowl to cool. Once the caramelized onions are finished cooking, transfer them to a plate to cool as well.

Preheat the oven to 400°F (205°C) and lightly grease a baking sheet with vegetable oil.

Unwrap the puff pastry and press out any folds. Cut the pastry into 8 squares, each approximately 4 × 4 inches (10 × 10 cm). Keep a small bowl of water nearby. Melt the butter in a small bowl in the microwave or a small skillet on the stove.

Working with 1 pastry square at a time, spoon 2 tablespoons of the potato filling onto the center of the square. Top with 1 tablespoon of the caramelized onions. Using your finger, dab water along the four edges of the pastry. Fold the pastry square in half diagonally, creating a triangle. Pinch the seams of the triangle to ensure the pastry sticks together. Using a pastry brush or your fingers, coat the top of the samosa with melted butter. Place the filled samosa on the prepared baking sheet. Repeat with the remaining pastry squares, potato filling, and onions.

Bake the samosas for 15 minutes, or until golden brown. Serve warm or at room temperature with Red and Green Chutneys.

Corn with Puffed Rice

BHEL

Bhel (puffed rice) tastes and acts similar to crispy rice cereals or Chex. Its neutral taste acts as a blank canvas for a variety of chutneys and chaat masala. Bhel puri mix (which has bhel and mathri, a wheat cracker) is readily available in the snack aisle of Indian stores, among the chips and crackers. Adding corn and red bell pepper to bhel gives it a fresh, salad-like composition, making it the ideal side or chai snack. Top everything off with sev, thin fried besan noodles also found in Indian markets.

SERVES 3 TO 6

- 1 cup (145 g) fresh or frozen corn kernels
- 1 tablespoon olive oil
- 1 teaspoon table salt
- 1 small red onion (125 g), peeled
- 1 red bell pepper, stem, ribs, and seeds removed
- ¼ cup (10 g) chopped fresh cilantro, stems included
- 4 cups (160 g) bhel puri mix
- 2 teaspoons chaat masala
- ¼ cup (60 g) Green Chutney (page 134)
- ¼ cup (60 g) Red Chutney (page 136)
- ¼ cup (30 g) sev, for garnish

Start by prepping the corn. Heat a cast-iron or nonstick skillet over medium heat and add the corn kernels, oil, and salt. Cook the corn for 5 to 7 minutes, letting it brown slightly. Transfer to a plate and let it cool.

Finely mince the onion and bell pepper, and transfer them to a serving bowl. Add the cilantro, along with the cooled corn and bhel puri mix. Top the bhel with the chaat masala, and green and red chutneys. Using tongs or a large spoon, mix the bhel with the vegetables and chutney. Top with the sev and serve.

NOTE: *Bhel should be served immediately so it remains crispy. Consume it the same day because leftovers get soggy, but you can prep the ingredients in advance and mix them when you are ready to serve.*

Heirloom Tomato and Fruit Chaat

Fruit chaat is a fresh reprieve from the fried and carb-heavy snacks of chai time. Fruit chaat is essentially a fruit salad, but with crispy toppings and chaat masala (flavored salt) to contrast the fruits' sweetness. It comes together in 5 minutes and can be made with any seasonal fruit. Many varieties of chaat masala exist, but they are all composed of amchoor (dried mango powder) for tang and kala namak (black salt) for umami. Pomegranates, grapes, kiwis, mangoes, and pears all make for delicious fruit chaat contenders.

SERVES 4 TO 6

2 tomatoes, preferably heirloom (360 g)

1 dragon fruit

1 apple

3 blood oranges

1 lemon

2 teaspoons chunky chaat masala

¼ cup (30 g) sev

Cut the tomatoes into ½-inch (1 cm) slices and arrange on a serving platter. Cut the dragon fruit in half lengthwise and scoop the flesh out of each half. Slice the dragon fruit flesh into ½-inch (1 cm) slices and place on top of the tomatoes. Core the apple, slice it ½-inch (1 cm) thick, and add to the platter.

Using a sharp paring knife, cut the peel and pith off the oranges. Slice the oranges into wedges between the membranes and remove the seeds (if any), then add them to the salad. Slice the lemon in half; squeeze one half over the salad and cut the other half into wedges for serving.

Sprinkle the chaat masala and sev over the chaat. Serve immediately to prevent the sev from getting soggy.

Mealify It

› Boiled and diced potatoes and/or drained and rinsed chickpeas can be added to the chaat to make it heartier.

How to Host a Chai Party

Chai parties can be as elaborate or simple as you like—their primary intent is to bring your friends and family together. Indians love to invite friends over for chai during those lazy afternoon hours that are too late for lunch but too early for dinner. The result? Jovial hours of eating endless rounds of chaat and small bites that may leave you stuffed for the rest of the evening.

A well-crafted chai party involves a spread of sweets and savories and lots of crunchy elements to accompany your tea. You can put out a cheese plate, crackers, and grapes. Any namkeen (dry fried snacks) from the Indian store can be served too. Start off with Oat Milk Chai (page 38) and some fruits and chips on the table. You can slice fruit for Heirloom Tomato and Fruit Chaat (page 57) using whatever you have in the fridge. While the Oat Milk Chai is sweetened, chai is traditionally served to guests unsweetened with a bowl of granulated sugar and a jar of honey on the side so guests can sweeten their tea to their liking.

To set yourself up for success, start preparing your chai party a few hours before your guests arrive. The chai can simmer on the stove for hours, or even be made a day ahead and stored in the fridge, then reheated in a pot on the stove; just make sure to keep it partially covered to prevent too much evaporation, or else it will taste too potent. If you do not want to deal with the hassle of live frying while guests are over, make the pakoras or piyajus in advance and store them in the oven at 200°F (95°C) to keep them crispy. If you prepare the onion and potato fillings ahead of time, you can quickly thaw some puff pastry to make Caramelized Onion and Potato Patties (page 51) or use the potato filling for Potato Patties with Pomegranate-Radish Salad (page 63). Masala Yams with Ramp Chimichurri (page 59) also work well—you can make the green sauce the night before and roast the yams first thing in the morning. Corn with Puffed Rice (page 54) should be mixed right before your guests arrive to prevent sogginess.

Make chai time a welcoming break with your guests, letting the tea and snacks flow well into dinnertime and even beyond.

Masala Yams with Ramp Chimichurri

This dish is a play on the popular sweet potato chaat you can find at street food stalls across India, but with the addition of a zesty green ramp chimichurri. Using small Garnet yams makes the dish easy to serve and eat, and the combination of the chaat masala and chimichurri creates a salty sourness that offsets the sweetness of the yams. Ramps are garlicky-tasting greens that make an appearance in markets for a short time in the spring. If you are making this dish outside of ramp season, you can substitute an equal number of scallions. The ramp chimichurri is also delicious dotted onto Corn with Puffed Rice (page 54) and Heirloom Tomato and Fruit Chaat (page 57).

SERVES 4 TO 6; MAKES 2 CUPS (480 ML) CHIMICHURRI

YAMS

4 or 5 Garnet yams (sweet potatoes; about 5 ounces/135 g each), scrubbed

2 teaspoons chunky chaat masala

1 teaspoon table salt

1 teaspoon coarse-ground black pepper

2 tablespoons olive oil

CHIMICHURRI

1 medium bunch mint (about 2 ounces/50 g), leaves only

5 or 6 ramps, root ends trimmed

½ cup (120 ml) olive oil

1 jalapeño chile, stem removed

3 garlic cloves, peeled

1 large bunch fresh cilantro, stem ends trimmed

¼ cup (60 ml) red wine vinegar

1 teaspoon paprika

1 teaspoon ground coriander

Preheat the oven to 425°F (220°C).

Slice each yam in half lengthwise, then place on a baking sheet and sprinkle with the chaat masala, salt, pepper, and olive oil. Use your hands to thoroughly coat the yam pieces in the spices and oil. Bake for

(continued)

20 minutes, then flip the yams and bake for another 20 minutes, or until they are tender when poked with a fork and visibly browned.

While yams are in the oven, make the chimichurri. Place the mint leaves, ramps, olive oil, jalapeño, garlic, cilantro, vinegar, paprika, and coriander in a blender or food processor and pulse until the chimichurri is slightly chunky, not totally smooth.

Transfer the yams to a serving platter. Top with chimichurri, and serve warm or cold.

The ramp chimichurri can be stored in the fridge in an airtight container for up to 1 week—it may lose some of its color, but the flavor will remain the same.

Potato Patties with Pomegranate-Radish Salad

ALOO TIKKI

Potato patties (aloo tikki) are traditionally fried and accompanied by chutneys and raw onions. Here, a baked approach keeps the tikkis lighter while still endowing them with a uniquely crispy texture. The patties' texture is comparable to home fries—crispy on the outside and soft on the inside. Like other chaats, this dish is all about that crunch—breadcrumbs on the tikkis and pomegranate and raw daikon in the mooli ka lachha (grated radish salad) add the right bite.

MAKES ABOUT 6 TIKKIS; SERVES 6

3 russet potatoes, (about 5 ounces/140 g each), scrubbed

3 teaspoons table salt

1 jalapeño chile, stem removed

¼ cup (10 g) chopped fresh cilantro, stem ends trimmed off

2 tablespoons all-purpose flour

2 tablespoons vegetable oil, plus more for greasing

1 teaspoon amchoor (dried mango powder)

1 teaspoon ground cumin

1 teaspoon ground coriander

1 teaspoon red chili powder

1 cup (110 g) dried breadcrumbs

Pomegranate-Radish Salad (page 129), for serving

Sev, for garnish

Start by preparing the potatoes. Put potatoes in a large pot and fill it with water at least 2 inches (5 cm) above the potatoes. Add 2 teaspoons of the salt, cover the pot with a lid, and bring the water to a boil over medium heat. Cook the potatoes for 20 minutes, or until fork-tender. Drain the potatoes in a colander and run them under cold water for 5 minutes to stop the cooking. Place the potatoes in the fridge to continue cooling.

(continued)

Mince the jalapeño, seeds and all. Put the jalapeño and cilantro in a large mixing bowl, along with the flour, oil, amchoor, cumin, coriander, red chili powder, and the remaining 1 teaspoon salt. Peel the potatoes with your hands, discarding the peels. Add the potatoes to the bowl. Mash everything together with a fork or your hands until the potatoes are thoroughly crumbled and the mixture is cohesive.

Preheat the oven to 350°F (175°C). Line a baking sheet with parchment paper and lightly grease the parchment with vegetable oil. Put the breadcrumbs in a shallow bowl or 13 × 9-inch (33 × 23 cm) rimmed baking sheet.

Grease your hands with the oil and scoop about 3 tablespoons of the potato mixture into your palm and form a round patty with your hands. The tikki should hold its shape—if it does not, mash the potato mixture further. Place the tikki in the breadcrumbs, gently pressing and flipping it to ensure the crumbs adhere to both sides, and place onto the prepared baking sheet. Repeat until the potato mixture is finished; you should have about 6 tikkis.

Bake the tikkis 15 minutes, or until they are golden brown. Remove the baking sheet from the oven, flip the tikkis over, then bake for another 15 minutes, or until the tikkis are deeply browned and slightly crispy to the touch.

Serve each tikki in an individual bowl, topped with pomegranate-radish salad and a sprinkle of sev.

Mains & Curries

Indian vegan main dishes vary from roasted, charred vegetables like whole okra and mushrooms to saucy proteins like stewed lentils and chole (chickpeas). But any vegetable in your fridge can be sautéed with onions, garlic, and chiles to make sabzis—aromatic veggie stir-fries. Pair these recipes with flatbreads and basmati rice for a satisfying complete meal.

Stuffed Okra and Eggplant

Bharwa (stuffing) is a treatment given to okra and eggplants that keeps them whole while filling them with shredded coconut and spices. Roasting them instead of simmering the vegetables on the stove helps evaporate excess moisture and adds a crispy texture to complement their tender interior.

SERVES 4 TO 6

6 mini globe eggplants (about 1 ounce/30 g each)

5 to 6 ounces (155 g) fresh okra pods

¼ cup (60 ml) olive oil

2 tablespoons unsweetened dried shredded coconut

2 teaspoons Garam Masala (page 146, or store-bought)

1 teaspoon red chili powder

1 teaspoon amchoor (dried mango powder)

1 teaspoon ground coriander

1 teaspoon ground cumin

1 teaspoon kosher salt

½ teaspoon ground turmeric

3 garlic cloves, peeled

Go-To Lentil Curry (page 88), for serving

Whole Wheat Flatbread (page 110), for serving

Begin by preparing the vegetables for stuffing. Slice a deep cross into the bottom (blossom end) of the eggplants; be careful to not cut all the way through. The stem end of the eggplant should remain intact. Slit each pod of okra lengthwise without splitting the pod in half. The slice should form a pocket that you'll be able to push your stuffing into.

Preheat the oven to 400°F (205°C).

Make the spice mix to stuff the veggies. Combine the olive oil, coconut, garam masala, red chili powder, amchoor, coriander, cumin, salt, and turmeric in a mixing bowl. Slice the garlic crosswise into thin chips and set aside.

(continued)

Spoon ½ teaspoon of the spice mix into the slit of each okra, and use your fingers to spread it inside the entirety of the pod. (Wear gloves to prevent the turmeric from staining your hands.) Gently open up the quartered eggplant and coat the inside of the eggplant with a thin layer of the spice mix with a pastry brush or your fingers.

Place the eggplants and okra pods in a 13 × 9-inch (33 × 23 cm) baking dish so they touch but do not overlap. Pour any remaining spice mix over the vegetables, and evenly distribute the garlic slices on top.

Bake for 15 minutes, until the vegetables are a deep golden brown and the spices are noticeably fragrant. Flip the vegetables over and bake for another 15 minutes, or until the vegetables are fork-tender all the way through.

Transfer the eggplant and okra to a serving plate. Serve hot with the lentil curry and whole wheat flatbread.

Rasam Cabbage Rolls

Rasam is a tangy, spicy tomato and tamarind broth commonly cooked in South India. Chefs often dress up this soup with pineapple, heaps of garlic, lentils, and chiles. Here, it is used as a base liquid to steam stuffed cabbage rolls. Many cultures around the world have their own version of stuffed cabbage; this version calls for spiced lentils and rice rolled and cooked in tender savoy cabbage leaves.

SERVES 4 TO 6

6 garlic cloves, peeled

3 medium Roma tomatoes

2 teaspoons vegetable oil

1 teaspoon black mustard seeds

½ teaspoon cumin seeds

¼ teaspoon ground turmeric

1 dried red chili

6 to 8 fresh curry leaves, stems removed

1½ teaspoons table salt

1 tablespoon tamarind concentrate

½ teaspoon cracked black pepper

6 cups (1.4 L) water

½ cup (20 g) chopped fresh cilantro

1 medium savoy or napa cabbage (about 10.5 ounces/300 g)

½ cup (95 g) yellow lentils, such as ahrar or moong daal

½ cup (90 g) basmati rice

Chili Oil (page 143), for serving

Slice the garlic crosswise into thin chips. Finely mince the tomatoes, chopping them as small as possible.

Pour the oil into a Dutch oven or large, heavy-bottomed pot and place it over medium heat. Add the mustard seeds, cumin seeds, turmeric, red chili, and curry leaves and toast them for 1 to 2 minutes. The spices should be crackling and aromatic. Add the tomatoes, 1 teaspoon of the salt, and the garlic. Cook for 5 to 6 minutes, until the water is cooked off and you are left with a thick, concentrated paste. It should be dark red in color.

Add the tamarind concentrate and pepper and combine into the tomato paste. Fry the paste for 1 minute, until it is fragrant and sizzling. Stir in the water and cilantro. Bring the rasam to a boil, then reduce the heat to medium-low. Simmer the rasam for 5 minutes, until it is maroon and fragrant.

(continued)

Next, prepare the stuffed cabbage rolls. Bring a large pot of water to a boil over high heat. Have a large, deep skillet at the ready.

Remove 6 to 8 of the outer leaves of the cabbage, slicing them off from where they are attached to the base. Make sure to keep the leaves intact. Remove any hard, white stem parts on the bottom. Add the cabbage leaves to the boiling water and boil for 1 minute to soften. Use tongs to remove them from the pot. Pat them dry with paper towels or a clean kitchen towel.

To make the cabbage roll stuffing, combine the lentils and rice in a large fine-mesh sieve. Rinse them under cold water until the water runs clear. Use your hands to stir and move the lentils and rice around to wash away more starch. Drain well and transfer them to a medium mixing bowl; add the remaining ½ teaspoon salt, and combine thoroughly.

Working with 1 cabbage leaf at a time, lay it cupped side up on a cutting board or clean work surface. Place a heaping tablespoon of the rice and lentil mixture in the middle of the leaf. (Do not overstuff the leaf, because the filling will expand during cooking.) Fold the sides of the cabbage leaf inward, toward the filling. Roll up the leaf lengthwise like a burrito. Place the cabbage rolls in a skillet, seam side down. The rolls should be tightly packed with each other and not overlapping.

Pour the rasam over the cabbage rolls and set the skillet on the stove over medium heat. Bring to a boil, then cover the pan and reduce the heat to low. The rasam should be simmering. Steam the rolls for 35 minutes, until fork-tender; the rice and lentils should be soft.

Plate the cabbage rolls in a deep serving dish and pour the remaining rasam over them. Top with Chili Oil and serve.

The rolls can be stored in the fridge in an airtight container for up to 3 days. Reheat in the microwave, or simmer on the stove for 5 minutes.

Tofu Tikka

Tikka is classically made by marinating pieces of a protein in yogurt and spices, then cooking them in a tandoor (stone oven). A hot home oven mimics the tandoor here, and plant-based yogurt provides the same creaminess and tang as the original. Tofu can taste bland if not seasoned well, so it is important to marinate it properly; make sure it sits for a minimum of 2 hours—but overnight is even better.

SERVES 4

1 cup (240 g) unsweetened cashew yogurt

1 teaspoon ground turmeric

1 teaspoon red chili powder

1 teaspoon Garam Masala (page 146, or store-bought)

1 teaspoon kosher salt

Juice of ½ lemon

3 garlic cloves, peeled

1-inch (2.5 cm) piece fresh ginger, peeled

2 blocks (14 to 16 ounces/ 400 to 450 g each) extra firm tofu

1 large red onion, peeled

1 red bell pepper, stem, ribs, and seeds removed

Red Chutney (page 136), for serving

Green Chutney (page 134), for serving

Combine the yogurt, turmeric, red chili powder, garam masala, salt, and lemon juice in a large mixing bowl. Using a Microplane or grater, grate the garlic and ginger into the marinade. Stir to combine thoroughly.

Pat the tofu dry and cut into 2 × 2-inch (5 × 5 cm) squares. Cut the onion in 1-inch-thick (2.5 cm) slices, then each slice into quarters. Cut the bell pepper into 1 × 1-inch (2.5 × 2.5 cm) squares. Add the tofu, onion, and bell pepper to the marinade and combine thoroughly. Cover the bowl with plastic wrap and place in the fridge for at least 2 hours or up to overnight.

(continued)

Preheat the oven to 425°F (220°C). Line a baking sheet with parchment paper.

Thread the vegetables and tofu onto skewers, alternating pieces of tofu, bell pepper, and onion. Leave a ¼-inch (6 mm) gap between the pieces. Place the skewers on the lined baking sheet.

Bake the skewers for 15 minutes, then flip them over. Bake for another 10 minutes, or until the tofu is crispy and the marinade dry. Some charred bits are encouraged. Serve hot with Red and Green Chutneys.

Massaman Lentil Curry

MASSAMAN DAAL

Lentils (daal) turn creamy and tender when simmered, and pair deliciously with the punch that is homemade massaman curry paste. Coconut milk imparts an extra-rich mouthfeel to the lentils, making this dish a true fusion between Indian and Thai food. Daal should be served with plain steamed basmati rice, Rice Pilaf (page 102), or Whole Wheat Flatbread (page 110). Use any leftover curry paste to make any vegetable curry, or as a marinade for roasted vegetables.

SERVES 4; MAKES ABOUT ½ CUP (100 G) CURRY PASTE

MASSAMAN CURRY PASTE

1 stalk lemongrass, white part only

2 shallots, peeled

4 garlic cloves, peeled

1-inch (2.5 cm) piece fresh ginger, peeled

1 fresh red chile, stem removed

1 tablespoon soy sauce

2 teaspoons brown sugar

½ teaspoon Garam Masala (page 146, or store-bought)

Juice of 1 lime

1 tablespoon vegetable oil (optional)

DAAL

1 tablespoon vegetable oil

1 cup (190 g) masoor daal (red lentils)

3 cups (720 ml) water

1 can (13.5 ounces/400 ml) full-fat coconut milk

1½ teaspoons table salt, or to taste

Chopped fresh cilantro, for garnish

Chili Oil (page 143), for garnish

Rice Pilaf (page 102), for serving

Prepare the lemongrass by removing the hard base of the stalk and a few of the outer layers of the bulb. You should be left with a soft piece of the bulb.

(continued)

Heat a cast-iron saucepan or Dutch oven over medium heat. Place the lemongrass, shallots, garlic, ginger, and chile in the pan. (The goal is to dry-roast and slightly char them to bring out their flavor.) Allow each vegetable to char for 1 to 2 minutes on each side. They should have some dark, almost burnt spots, and be aromatic.

Place the charred vegetables, soy sauce, brown sugar, garam masala, and lime juice in a blender or food processor. Blend into a smooth paste. If the blender gets stuck, add vegetable oil ½ teaspoon at a time to help get it going again. Transfer the paste to a glass jar.

Heat a Dutch oven or wok over medium heat with 1 tablespoon vegetable oil. Add 2 tablespoons of the curry paste to the oil and fry, stirring occasionally, for 2 to 3 minutes. The paste will darken and lose some water. Add the lentils and stir to completely coat them with the curry paste.

Stir in the water and coconut milk. Bring the daal to a simmer, then reduce the heat to low. Cook for 12 to 15 minutes, until the lentils are fully soft. Mix in salt to taste.

Transfer the daal to a serving bowl and top with chopped cilantro and Chili Oil. Serve with Rice Pilaf.

Store the leftover curry paste in the fridge in a tightly capped jar for up to 2 weeks.

All-Day Chickpea Curry

CHOLE

The best way to cook beans is low and slow—as in, over low heat and spending lots of time on the stove. Pressure cookers do make cooking chole (chickpeas) quick and easy, but low and slow on the stove for hours results in a deep flavor and tender bean unmatched by any expedited method. This recipe can easily be made with kidney beans or black-eyed peas if you prefer—any dense brown bean will result in a delicious chole. If you remember and have the time, soak the beans in advance for at least 8 hours. This will cut the cooking time down by an hour, but it is no big deal if you forget.

SERVES 6

- 4 garlic cloves, peeled
- 1-inch (2.5 cm) piece fresh ginger, peeled
- 2 medium Roma tomatoes
- 1 medium red or white onion, peeled
- 1 tablespoon vegetable oil
- 1 cinnamon stick
- 1 dried bay leaf
- ½ teaspoon whole cloves
- ½ teaspoon green cardamom pods
- 2 teaspoons table salt
- 2 teaspoons Garam Masala (page 146, or store-bought)
- 1 teaspoon amchoor (dried mango powder)
- 2 cups (370 g) dried chickpeas
- 6 cups (1.4 L) water
- 1 black tea bag
- 1 jalapeño chile, stem removed
- ½ cup (20 g) minced fresh cilantro, for garnish
- Rice Pilaf (page 102), for serving
- Pickled Onions (page 130), for serving

Finely mince the garlic and ginger, chopping them so small that they almost form a paste. Chop the tomatoes and onion finely as well.

Pour the oil into a Dutch oven or large, heavy-bottomed pot and set it over medium heat. Add the cinnamon stick, bay leaf, cloves, and cardamom pods and cook for 1 to 2 minutes, until they are crackling and aromatic. Add the garlic, ginger, onion, tomatoes, and 1 teaspoon of the salt and stir constantly until the mixture has lost all its water and formed a dark red paste. Stir the garam masala and amchoor into the paste, frying for 1 minute, until the spices brown and become fragrant.

Add the chickpeas, water, tea bag, and the remaining teaspoon salt. Bring to a boil, then reduce the heat to medium-low. The water should be at a simmer. Cover half of the pot with a lid. Every 30 minutes or so, stir the chole to prevent them from sticking to the bottom of the pot. If the water has mostly evaporated and is not covering the chole, add more, 1 cup (240 ml) at a time. Cook the beans for about 3 hours, until they are completely tender and falling apart in your mouth when you taste one. If they are still al dente, add another ½ cup (120 ml) water and cook for another 30 minutes.

Remove and discard the bay leaf, cinnamon stick, and tea bag. Thinly slice the jalapeño and add it to the chole. Using the back of a serving spoon, smash about one-quarter of the beans to thicken the curry. Add more salt to taste.

Transfer the chole to a serving dish and top with the cilantro. Serve with Rice Pilaf and Pickled Onions.

Chole can be stored in the fridge in an airtight container for up to 4 days. Reheat in the microwave for 4 minutes, or on the stove over low heat until the curry is bubbling.

Spinach with Whole Roasted Cauliflower

PALAK GOBI

Roasting a whole head of cauliflower (gobi) is a surprisingly simple task that will impress at any dinner party. The key to a tender and flavorful vegetable is time—the cauliflower head takes over an hour to roast in the oven, which results in a buttery interior and crunchy exterior. The spinach curry carries all the flavor of the dish—the spinach (palak) is fragrant with turmeric and a touch of red chili powder, and made rich with the addition of cashew cream. The magic of this dish is in its presentation: The whole cauliflower head looks regal sitting in the middle of a dining table. Serve with plain steamed basmati rice, Rice Pilaf (page 102), or Whole Wheat Flatbread (page 110).

SERVES 4

1 small to medium cauliflower (½ to ¾ pound/250-350 g)

4 tablespoons (½ stick/60 g) salted plant-based butter

2 teaspoons table salt

½ teaspoon ground turmeric

½ teaspoon red chili powder

½ teaspoon cracked black pepper

4 cups (80 g) fresh baby spinach, leaves only, rinsed but not completely dried

1 cup (150 g) Masala Cashew Cream (page 140)

2 tablespoons warm water

Preheat the oven to 400°F (205°C).

Remove any leaves on the cauliflower, and cut off most of the stem so the bottom is flat and the cauliflower is able to sit upright.

Put the butter in a small heat-proof bowl and melt in the microwave for 30 seconds, or in a small skillet on the stove over low heat. Add 1 teaspoon

(continued)

of the salt, the turmeric, red chili powder, and black pepper and combine thoroughly. Place the cauliflower on a baking sheet. Using your hands or a pastry brush, coat the entire cauliflower head with the spiced butter, making sure to get the butter into the crevices of the vegetable.

Loosely cover the cauliflower with aluminum foil. (The foil will help the cauliflower steam and become tender all the way through.) Bake for 45 minutes. Remove the foil and bake for another 30 minutes. The cauliflower should be golden brown and crispy on the outside. Pierce the cauliflower with a fork to see if it is tender all the way through. If not, return it to the oven for 5 to 10 minutes.

While the cauliflower is in the oven, prepare the spinach curry. Cook the spinach with the remaining 1 teaspoon salt in a Dutch oven or large saucepan over medium heat. Allow the spinach to fully wilt and lose most of its water; this takes 5 to 6 minutes. Transfer the spinach along with ¾ cup (75 g) of the cashew cream to a blender and pulse until smooth. Pour the curry back into the pan and simmer for 2 minutes, stirring frequently, until the curry has slightly thickened.

Pour the curry into a deep serving dish and place the roasted cauliflower in the center. Thin the remaining ¼ cup (25 g) cashew cream with the water and drizzle it over the cauliflower and spinach. Serve warm.

The Daal Glossary

Daal—lentils, pulses, and legumes—is the most prolific protein in South Asian cooking. Whether it's simmered in a stew, toasted dry to add a crunch to porridges, or blended into a crispy batter for fritters, daal is ubiquitous across Indian recipes for any meal of the day. The term "daal" refers to the original form of the lentil, but is also synonymous with the stew that is made from cooking lentils. The stew has a common flavor base no matter which legume you choose. The cooking time of each daal depends on its size, with bigger beans needing more time to fully tenderize, but they all come together in the end to form a velvety, creamy curry.

All daals start with a base of sautéed onions, ginger, garlic, and tomatoes, cooked with salt until the tomatoes have completely broken down and formed a paste. This "Indian sofrito" then mingles with cumin, red chili powder, dried mango powder (amchoor), and coriander to flavor the base. For yellow daals like ahrar and moong, turmeric is added to enhance their color, but I like to add it to all daals for its earthy flavor. Dried lentils, salt, and water are then added and cooked with the spiced sofrito until the daal reaches a tender, velvety texture. Daal is often topped with tempered oil and spices (tadka), such as Chili Oil (page 143). Serve daal with steamed rice or Whole Wheat Flatbread (page 110).

A traditional way of cooking daal is in a pressure cooker, but you can also do a slow boil in a big pot, which enhances the flavor and texture of the dish. Cooking the daal at a high pressure leaves it flavorless and waterlogged; the lentils do not get the time they need to absorb the spices and flavors of the sofrito. Though slowly boiling the daal takes longer, the pulses meld with the aromatics, leading to a more complex bite. The stew is imbued with the starches the lentils release, leaving a thick stock that coats your mouth. If you soak the dried daal for an hour or two before cooking, it reduces the cooking time of the daal and improves its digestibility.

When it comes to choosing a daal, your options range from tough-skinned, dark kidney beans to pearly, iridescent split peas. A visit to the pantry aisle in an Indian store may leave you overwhelmed—lentils of vibrant reds, greens, and tans glisten like small jewels. Each legume here has a Hindi name that will help you identify it in the grocery store, but the key things to learn and practice are the sizes and colors of the lentils. A few simple rules will help you transform any dried pulse into a creamy, savory daal.

MASOOR DAAL

These lentils are sometimes red, sometimes brown, depending on whether the skin has been left on. They are some of the smallest lentils, making them ideal for fast cooking. The "unwashed" version, with the skin intact, has not only a higher nutritional value (from its higher fiber content), but also the distinct texture of a chewy, slightly tough exterior that gives way to a melty, soft lentil on the inside. Reach for masoor daal when you want a quick, hearty option that absorbs the flavor of spices well.

AHRAR DAAL

These split pigeon peas, also called toor daal, are larger yellow pulses often found split in half, without their skins. Their ability to absorb tomato and spices and their chewy mouthfeel make them regulars in stews like sambar (a South Indian lentil stew) and daal tadka (lentils with tempered oil and spices). Ahrar daal is sweeter than its other legume counterparts, making it a tasty vehicle for spicy vegetables and pickles.

MOONG DAAL

Split green lentils, or moong, are small ovals with a jade-like hue. Among the smallest of the daals, these are ideal to cook mixed with basmati rice because they have a similar absorbency and therefore cook time. To make khichdi (rice-lentil porridge), start with the "Indian sofrito" described above; add 1 cup each of rice and daal, then follow the cooking instructions in Go-To Lentil Curry (page 88). "Unwashed" moong, with the skin on, has the most distinct texture of the daals due to the chewy, earthy skin.

URAD DAAL

Also called black gram lentils, urad has a mild taste that pairs well with fats and oils, and is most commonly found in daal makhani (lentils with butter and cream). To make urad daal makhani plant-based, follow the steps in Go-To Lentil Curry (page 88), adding Masala Cashew Cream (page 140) in the last 10 minutes of cooking. Simmer the cream with the daal to make a buttery, velvety curry.

CHANA DAAL

Here the daal selection may start to get confusing: Chana daal is also yellow, and chana also can mean mature chickpeas—chana daal is chickpeas, but a smaller, tougher version also called black chickpeas. The skin is removed from these chickpeas and they are split in two, revealing large half-moon legumes. What sets chana daal apart from other yellow daals is its size and matte texture; it's bigger than ahrar and urad and has the grainiest, heartiest texture of the daals. Chana daal takes the longest to cook due to its size and density; a 3- to 4-hour soak in water will help it break down and soften faster when cooking.

Go-To Lentil Curry

DAAL

The dozens of varieties of lentils—green, red, black, French, peeled, and more—can be overwhelming. The choices may seem daunting, but each lentil can be cooked into a daal. Daal (which literally means "lentil") also refers to an aromatic curry that can be eaten on its own like a soup or paired with rice and vegetables for a full meal. Skinless yellow and red lentils tend to be more tender and smoother than the heartier brown and black varieties. Mix multiple types for a daal with multiple textures.

SERVES 4

4 garlic cloves, peeled

1-inch (2.5 cm) piece fresh ginger, peeled

2 medium Roma tomatoes

1 medium red or white onion, peeled

1 fresh green chile pepper, stem removed

2 teaspoons vegetable oil

2 teaspoons table salt

1 teaspoon ground cumin

1 teaspoon ground coriander

1 teaspoon amchoor (dried mango powder)

½ teaspoon ground turmeric

1 cup (about 190 g) lentils of your choice

4 cups (1 L) water

Chopped fresh cilantro, for garnish

Juice of ½ lemon, for garnish

Chili Oil (page 143), for garnish

Finely mince the garlic and ginger. Chop them so small that they almost form a paste. Chop the tomatoes, onion, and green chile finely as well.

Pour the oil into a large Dutch oven or heavy-bottomed pot and place it over medium heat. Add the garlic, ginger, onion, tomatoes, green chile, and 1 teaspoon of the salt and cook, stirring constantly, until the mixture has lost all its water and formed a dark red paste, about 5 minutes.

Stir in the cumin, coriander, amchoor, and turmeric and cook for 1 minute, until the spices are aromatic and the paste turns dark brown.

Add the lentils, water, and the remaining 1 teaspoon salt. Bring the daal to a simmer, then reduce the heat to low. Cook for 12 to 15 minutes, until the lentils are fully soft. (Larger lentils may take up to 20 minutes.)

Mix in more salt to taste. Transfer the daal to a serving bowl and top with cilantro, the lemon juice, and Chili Oil to taste. Serve hot.

Store leftover daal in an airtight container in the refrigerator for up to 4 days. To reheat, simmer on the stove for 5 minutes.

Brussels Sprouts Manchurian

Indian-Chinese food is a popular fusion cuisine found throughout India, and many of the dishes are plant-based. "Manchurian" dishes are fried cutlets of vegetables or paneer served in a gravy with the flavor of soy sauce, the sweetness of ketchup, and the aroma of garlic and ginger. This is a dry, slightly sticky version that pairs well with rice or can be served on its own. It is commonly made with cauliflower, but the layers of Brussels sprouts provide a more interesting texture—they get a great crisp when fried.

SERVES 4

FRIED BRUSSELS SPROUTS

1 pound (450 g) Brussels sprouts

4 cups (1 L) vegetable oil

¾ cup (95 g) all-purpose flour

⅓ cup (43 g) cornstarch

⅓ cup (80 ml) water

2 teaspoons table salt

1 teaspoon red chili powder

MANCHURIAN SAUCE

5 garlic cloves, peeled

1-inch (2.5 cm) piece fresh ginger, peeled

1 fresh green chile pepper, stem removed

2 tablespoons ketchup

1 tablespoon soy sauce

1 tablespoon sriracha

1 teaspoon rice vinegar

1 teaspoon brown sugar

1 tablespoon toasted sesame oil

1 green bell pepper, stem, ribs, and seeds removed

1 large white onion, peeled

2 green onions (scallions), root ends trimmed, thinly sliced, for garnish

2 teaspoons sesame seeds, for garnish

Rice Pilaf (page 102) or steamed basmati rice, for serving

Trim the stems of the Brussels sprouts and remove any damaged outer leaves. Slice each Brussels sprout in half lengthwise.

(continued)

Heat the vegetable oil in a large Dutch oven, wok, or cast-iron pot over medium heat for 10 to 15 minutes, until it reaches 350°F (175°C).

Combine the flour, cornstarch, water, 1 teaspoon of the salt, and the red chili powder in a large mixing bowl. Fully mix with a spoon so no lumps remain. The texture of the batter should not be too thin or runny. If it feels like there is too much liquid, add more flour 1 tablespoon at a time. Add the cut Brussels sprouts to the batter, and use your hands or the spoon to fully coat them with the batter.

Set up your frying station: Have a plate lined with paper towels ready. If you don't have a deep-frying thermometer, to check if the oil is hot enough to start frying, drop a small bit of the batter into the pot; if it immediately rises and starts to crackle, the oil is ready.

Working in batches, use a slotted spoon or spider to scoop up batter-coated pieces of Brussels sprouts and gently drop them into the oil. Fry for 2 minutes on each side—they should be golden brown all over. Move the pieces around with the slotted spoon to ensure they are not sticking together. Using a clean spoon or spider, transfer the Brussels sprouts to the paper towel–lined plate. Repeat until you have fried all the Brussels sprouts. After you have fried all the sprouts, sprinkle the remaining 1 teaspoon salt over them.

To make the sauce, finely mince the garlic, ginger, and green chile. Put them in a small mixing bowl and add the ketchup, soy sauce, sriracha, rice vinegar, brown sugar, and sesame oil. Thoroughly combine with a spoon or spatula. Chop the bell pepper and onion into 1-inch (2.5 cm) pieces.

Pour the sauce into a large wok or deep skillet and set it over medium heat. Cook for 2 minutes, until bubbling and thick. Add the bell pepper and onion to the sauce and stir to coat them completely. Cook the vegetables with the sauce for 3 to 4 minutes, until they start to soften. Add the Brussels sprouts and mix fully with the sauce. Cook just until they are heated through.

Transfer everything to a serving dish. Sprinkle the green onions and sesame seeds on the Brussels sprouts and serve with Rice Pilaf.

Mushroom Dry Curry

MUSHROOM SABZI

Sabzis (cooked vegetable dishes) are the basis of all Indian dinners—you will find dry and gravy-based vegetable dishes accompanying daals and pickles. Here you fry mushrooms until their edges are crisped before turning them into a sabzi. Patience is the key to texturally pleasing mushrooms—frying them untouched helps them crisp and get that desired golden brown color. When cleaning the mushrooms, avoid washing them—mushrooms absorb water quickly, which prevents them from getting crispy. Instead, use a paper towel to brush away any dirt.

SERVES 4

1 pound (450 g) mixed mushrooms, such as oyster mushrooms, cremini mushrooms, and shiitake mushrooms, trimmed and cleaned

2 teaspoons vegetable oil

3 garlic cloves, peeled

½ medium red onion, peeled

1 fresh green chile pepper, stem removed

1 teaspoon cumin seeds

1 teaspoon ground turmeric

1 teaspoon red chili powder

1 teaspoon amchoor (dried mango powder)

1 teaspoon ground coriander

1 teaspoon table salt

Chopped fresh cilantro, for garnish

Lemon wedges, for serving

Tear or cut the mushrooms into even pieces, about 1 inch (2.5 cm).

Heat a large nonstick or cast-iron skillet over medium-high heat and brush the inside with 1 teaspoon of the vegetable oil. Working in batches if needed, arrange an even layer of mushrooms in the pan with minimal overlapping. Cook the mushrooms for 5 minutes untouched, then flip them and cook on the other side for another 5 minutes, until golden brown and crispy. Transfer the mushrooms to a plate.

(continued)

Finely mince the garlic, onion, and chile pepper. Add the remaining 1 teaspoon oil to the pan along with the garlic, onion, and chile. Cook until the garlic and onion become translucent, about 4 minutes. Add the cumin, turmeric, red chili powder, amchoor, and coriander and mix thoroughly. Return all the mushrooms to the pan, add the salt, and combine everything fully. Cook the sabzi for 3 to 4 minutes, until the spices are evenly distributed and mushrooms are browned.

Transfer the sabzi to a serving dish. Top with cilantro and serve with lemon wedges on the side.

The Sabzi Formula

Sabzi literally means "vegetable dish." They are main dishes, and can be dry-sautéed or simmered in gravy; they sometimes include a protein like tofu or paneer. Use sabzis as a convenient and tasty excuse to clean out your fridge. You can throw a medley of vegetables together, or just use a wilted bunch of kale that needs to be eaten. If you keep a few key rules in mind, a sabzi is a "no-recipe" recipe you can pull out of your back pocket whenever the right opportunity—or vegetable—presents itself.

The most important lesson to learn when practicing sabzis is how to prepare the produce. Mistreating a vegetable can result in a too-tough bite of cauliflower or slimy piece of okra. For hearty greens like kale, mustard, or Swiss chard, remove the tough stems and tear or chop the tender leaves into 1-inch (2.5 cm) pieces; sauté them for 5 minutes with the aromatic base until they're soft. For root veggies like potatoes, beets, and carrots, first peel, dice, and boil them until fork-tender before adding them into the base. For delicate veggies like bell peppers, peas, and corn, just chop them to your desired size and cook for 5 minutes over medium heat with the base.

The base of all sabzis is similar—garlic, onions, and chiles. No matter what vegetable you choose, the process is the same. For every 1 pound (450 g) of produce, mince half a medium red onion and cook it in a little oil until translucent, about 4 minutes. Mince and add 3 garlic cloves and 1 fresh green chile pepper and cook for 2 minutes, until they are fragrant and slightly browned. A foolproof spice combination is 1 teaspoon each of cumin seeds, turmeric, red chili powder, amchoor, dried cilantro leaves, and salt: Cumin seeds create peppery flavor bombs in each bite. Turmeric colors the dish golden hues and adds a delicate, earthy flavor. Red chili powder spices things up and adds a smoky bite. A fresh jalapeño or another green chile can be swapped in for red chili powder when you want a fresher taste, or layer them both for an extra-spicy dish. Amchoor balances the spice with some tartness, but feel free to add an equal volume of lemon juice in its place. The dried cilantro leaves give it an herby finish. Add each component of the spice mix to the sautéed garlic, onions, and chiles, then toast the spices for 1 minute, until they are aromatic. If using lemon juice, add that at the very end of the cooking process, before taking the sabzi off the heat.

Jalapeño Butter Tofu

Eating plant-based does not have to mean missing out on the decadence of butter chicken. This adaptation employs cashews and plant-based butter to create the creamy gravy that makes this version of everyone's favorite Indian takeout order. Frying jalapeño slices in the butter imparts a much-desired spiciness to the sauce and helps cut into the richness.

SERVES 4

2 blocks (14 ounces/400 g each) firm tofu

2 tablespoons vegetable oil

2 cups (300 g) Masala Cashew Cream (page 140)

2 tablespoons (30 g) salted plant-based butter

1 jalapeño chile, stem removed

Chopped fresh cilantro, for garnish

Rice Pilaf (page 102), for serving

Garlic Confit Naan (page 113), for serving

Cut the tofu into 1-inch (2.5 cm) cubes. Pat dry any excess moisture with paper towels.

Heat a large nonstick skillet over medium-high heat for 4 to 5 minutes, until a drop of water on the surface evaporates immediately. Pour in the oil and swirl it around until it is shimmery and easily coats the bottom of the pan. Add a cube of tofu to the oil to check if it is ready; if the tofu sizzles right away, it is hot enough. Otherwise, wait another 2 to 3 minutes for the oil to continue heating.

Working in batches, add a layer of tofu cubes to the pan. Keep the cubes spaced apart so none are touching. Let them pan-fry for 5 minutes untouched. Flip them and let them crisp for another 5 minutes, until golden brown and crisp on both sides. Transfer the fried tofu to a large plate and repeat with the remaining cubes, adding more oil as needed.

Once all the tofu is fried, reduce the heat under the pan to medium-low and pour in the cashew cream. Bring to a simmer, then return the tofu

(continued)

cubes to the pan and combine fully. Cook the curry for 2 to 3 minutes, until it has deepened in color and thickened slightly. Transfer to a serving bowl.

Melt the butter in a small nonstick or cast-iron skillet over medium heat. Slice the jalapeño into ⅛-inch-thick (3 mm) slices. For a less spicy curry, discard the seeds. Add the jalapeño slices to the butter and cook for 1 minute, until they are fragrant and slightly browned.

Pour the jalapeño butter over the tofu curry and sprinkle with cilantro. Serve hot with Rice Pilaf and Garlic Confit Naan.

Grains & Breads

Learn to layer spices and aromatics in pots of pulao (rice pilaf) and how to laminate parathas (flatbread) like a pro. These Indian breads and rices not only make great accompaniments to your entrées and curries, but biryanis and kulchas can even shine as stand-alone meals.

Rice Pilaf

PULAO

Pulao is the basis of every North Indian meal. Add all the ingredients into one pot; the everyday spices imbue plain rice with a mouthwatering fragrance. Do not fret if you are missing any of the suggested spices; work with what you have.

SERVES 6

- **2 cups (360 g) white basmati rice**
- **1 tablespoon vegetable oil**
- **1 teaspoon cumin seeds**
- **½ teaspoon whole cloves**
- **1 dried bay leaf**
- **1 cinnamon stick**
- **½ cup (65 g) frozen or fresh green peas**
- **4 cups (1 L) water**
- **1 teaspoon table salt**

Place the rice in a fine-mesh sieve and rinse under cold water until the water runs clear, using your hands to stir and move the rice around to wash away more starch. Drain well and set aside.

Heat the oil in a large pot over medium heat. After the oil has been heating for 2 minutes, add the cumin seeds, cloves, bay leaf, and cinnamon stick. Cook the spices for 1 to 2 minutes, until they are crackling and fragrant.

Add the rice and green peas and stir until they are fully coated with the oil and mixed with the spices. Stir in the water and salt. Reduce the heat to medium-low. After the water comes to a boil, reduce the heat to low and cover the pot.

Cook the rice for 20 minutes, until fluffy and all the water is absorbed, then shut off the heat. Let the covered pot sit for 5 minutes. Remove the lid and fluff the pulao with a fork. Serve hot.

Pulao can be stored in the fridge in an airtight container for up to 3 days. Reheat in the microwave for 3 to 4 minutes.

Meal-ify It

- Adding carrots and green beans to pulao makes an even heartier vegetable dish that will suffice for a whole meal. Add ½ cup (70 g) each frozen diced carrots and chopped green beans to the rice at the same time as the green peas. The carrots and beans will thaw and cook along with the peas.

Wild Mushroom Fried Rice

BIRYANI

Biryani, an opulent, one-pot meat and rice dish, gets the paella treatment in this version with tender mushrooms, lots of veggies, and a crispy bottom. Biryani is always customizable. Original Hyderabadi biryani is teeming with star anise, cardamom, and vegetables, but South Asians living across the world add their own flair and preparations according to regional ingredients and their own spice preferences. Use a wide, deep pan, such as a paella pan or cast-iron skillet, to guarantee a fluffy biryani set over a layer of crispy rice.

SERVES 4

2 cups (380 g) white basmati rice

1 pound (450 g) assorted mushrooms, such as shiitake, cremini, chanterelle, and king oyster, wiped clean with a paper towel

1 medium red onion, peeled

3 garlic cloves, peeled

1-inch (2.5 cm) piece fresh ginger, peeled

2 medium carrots, peeled

¼ cup (30 g) raw, unsalted cashews

2 tablespoons vegetable oil

½ cup (70 g) frozen or fresh green peas

2 teaspoons table salt

1 tablespoon Garam Masala (page 146, or store-bought)

1 tablespoon tomato paste

3½ cups (840 ml) water

Chopped fresh cilantro, for garnish

1 lemon, cut into wedges, for serving

Unsweetened plant-based yogurt, for serving

Place the rice in a fine-mesh sieve and rinse under cold water until the water runs clear, using your hands to stir and move the rice around to wash away more starch. Drain well and set aside. Tear or cut the mushrooms into ½-inch (1 cm) pieces. Mince the onion, garlic, and ginger. Cut carrots into ¼-inch-thick (6 mm) coins. Chop the cashews. Line a plate with paper towels.

(continued)

Heat 1 tablespoon of the oil in a wide, heavy-bottomed pan over medium heat. (A cast-iron skillet works well, and a paella pan is even better.) Add the mushrooms to the oil and fry them on one side, undisturbed, for 5 minutes. Flip the mushrooms and fry the other side for 5 minutes, until they are golden brown and crispy. Transfer the mushrooms to the prepared plate.

Add the remaining 1 tablespoon oil to the pan and add the onion, ginger, garlic, carrots, cashews, peas and salt. Cook and toss everything together until the aromatics are soft and brown, 5 to 6 minutes.

Add the garam masala and tomato paste and cook, stirring, for 3 minutes or until the tomato paste turns a deep shade of maroon brown.

Add the rice and water and stir to blend everything together. Allow the water to come to a simmer, then reduce the heat to low and cover the pan with a lid. Cook for 20 minutes, undisturbed.

Check the rice by testing a grain, smashing it between your fingers. The rice should be soft. If the rice is not fully cooked, sprinkle ½ cup water on the rice, replace the lid, and steam for an additional 5 minutes. Sprinkle the crisped mushrooms on top of the rice.

Sprinkle cilantro on top and serve the biryani directly out of the pan, with lemon wedges alongside and a bowl of yogurt for drizzling.

Lemon Rice

Cooked white rice, crunchy fried peanuts, and squeezes of fresh lemon juice are all you really need to make this iteration of what you could call "Indian fried rice." The spices and chana daal add a nutty crunch, but feel free to use whatever lentils you have in your pantry. Add peas or carrots to the rice to make it a full meal, or replace the peanuts with cashews for a milder nutty element. If you have leftover cooked rice, you'll need about 4 cups (800 g). Make sure it is separated and dry, and skip the first two steps, going straight to preparing the spices.

SERVES 4

2 cups (380 g) white basmati rice
3½ cups (840 ml) water
¼ cup (60 ml) vegetable oil
¼ cup (34 g) raw, unsalted peanuts
1 tablespoon chana daal
2 teaspoons black mustard seeds
¼ cup (10 g) fresh curry leaves, stems removed
4 or 5 dried red chilis
2 teaspoons table salt
½ teaspoon ground turmeric
¼ cup (60 ml) freshly squeezed lemon juice
Chopped fresh cilantro, for garnish

Place the rice in a fine-mesh sieve and rinse under cold water until the water runs clear, using your hands to stir and move the rice around to wash away more starch. Drain well.

Transfer the rice to a medium saucepan along with the water and place over medium heat. Allow the water to reach a slow boil, then reduce the heat to low and cover the pot. Cook the rice for 12 minutes, until the water is absorbed and the rice is fluffy, then turn off the heat. Let the rice sit, covered, for 5 minutes, then fluff with a fork. If the rice is not properly fluffed, it will become clumpy, so make sure it is separated and dry.

While the rice is cooking, prepare the spices. Heat the oil in a wok or wide nonstick skillet over medium heat. Add the peanuts, chana daal, mustard seeds, and curry leaves. Toast until the peanuts and chana daal are

(continued)

golden brown and fragrant. Add the dried chilis, salt, and turmeric and lightly toast them for 2 to 3 minutes, until aromatic.

Add the lemon juice and stir to dissolve the turmeric and salt. Let the juice come to a soft simmer. Add the rice and toss to combine thoroughly. If the rice was cold, cook until it is fully reheated. Transfer the rice to a bowl and serve hot, topped with cilantro.

Whole Wheat Flatbread

ROTI

Atta (Indian whole wheat flour) is finer than Western whole wheat flour, and lends a delicate texture that allows this dough to be rolled out very thin. Indians covet thin rotis to provide a simple vehicle for eating sabzis (vegetable dishes) and daal. Use atta dough to make paratha (layered flatbread; see page 115) as well as simple rotis (thin flatbreads). Rotis are best to eat with mains and curries, whereas thick and stuffed parathas can stand alone or be paired with pickles and a pat of butter.

MAKES 6 ROTIS

2 cups (240 g) atta flour (Indian whole wheat flour), plus more for rolling

½ cup (120 ml) water

1 tablespoon vegetable oil, plus more for greasing

1 teaspoon table salt

2 tablespoons (30 g) plant-based butter, for serving

Using your hands, combine the atta flour with the water, oil, and salt in a large mixing bowl. Knead the dough in the bowl for about 6 minutes, until it is smooth and supple. Cover and let the dough rest for 30 minutes.

Divide the dough into 6 equal pieces. Oil your palms lightly, and roll each piece of dough between them to create a small ball. Cover the balls with a clean kitchen towel to prevent them from drying out.

Lightly flour the countertop with atta. Working with one dough ball at a time, use your palm to slightly flatten the ball, then roll out the dough to an ⅛-inch-thick (3 mm) circle with a rolling pin. The roti should be 6 inches (15 cm) across. Repeat with each remaining dough ball, keeping the rotis separate so they do not stick together. Cover with a clean kitchen towel so they do not dry out.

Heat a nonstick skillet or tawa over medium-high heat. Transfer 1 roti to the pan with tongs and cook undisturbed for 3 to 4 minutes. The roti may start to inflate—let this happen; it will naturally deflate. Using the tongs, flip the roti and cook it for 2 minutes on the other side, until it takes on a light brown color with some charred spots. Wrap the cooked rotis in a clean kitchen towel to keep them warm. Repeat with the rest of the rotis.

Serve the rotis while hot with a small pat of butter on top of each one.

The uncooked dough can be stored in the fridge in an airtight container for up to 3 days. Cooked rotis can be wrapped in foil and stored in the fridge for up to 1 week, or in the freezer for up to 1 month. Reheat cooked rotis in a nonstick skillet for 1 minute on each side.

Garlic Confit Naan

Garlic naan is one of the most recognizable breads in Indian cuisine—it's a fluffy, tangy, and rich vehicle for delicious curry. Taking the extra step to confit the garlic injects the naan with even stronger yet sweeter notes of garlic without overpowering the subtle flavor of the naan. The naan can be enjoyed on its own or with any curry.

MAKES 6 NAANS

NAAN

1 cup (240 ml) warm (110° to 115°F/43° to 46°C) water

1 tablespoon granulated sugar

1 packet (2¼ teaspoons/7 g) active dry yeast

2 cups (250 g) all-purpose flour

½ cup (60 g) atta (Indian whole wheat flour), plus more for rolling

2 tablespoons vegetable oil, plus more for greasing

1 teaspoon table salt

Chopped fresh cilantro, for garnish

Flaky salt, for garnish

GARLIC CONFIT

1 cup (2 sticks/230 to 250 g) plant-based butter

1 cup (240 ml) olive oil

2 bulbs garlic, cloves separated and peeled (about 20 to 24 cloves)

1 teaspoon table salt

½ teaspoon cracked black pepper

Pour the water into a large mixing bowl or the bowl of a stand mixer. Sprinkle the sugar and yeast on top and stir to dissolve them. Wait 5 minutes for the yeast to bloom and bubble—it will look slightly puffed in appearance. If the yeast does not activate, start over with a new packet.

Add the all-purpose flour, atta flour, oil, and table salt to the yeast mixture and knead in the bowl by hand for 10 minutes, or fit the mixer with the dough hook attachment and mix for 8 minutes on medium speed. The dough should be supple and smooth. Transfer the ball of dough to a clean large mixing bowl and cover with plastic wrap or a clean kitchen towel. Set the bowl in a warm place and let the dough rise for 1 hour or until it is doubled in size.

(continued)

While the dough is rising, make the garlic confit. Melt the butter in a medium pot over medium-low heat. Add the olive oil, garlic, salt, and pepper. Once the mixture hits a soft simmer, reduce the heat to low. Cook for 30 to 40 minutes, until the garlic is totally soft and almost falling apart. Remove the garlic cloves from the oil and slightly mash them with a fork. Set aside the oil to top the naans or use as a fragrant dipping oil. Store the oil in the refrigerator and consume within 48 hours.

Lightly grease a baking sheet with vegetable oil. After the dough has risen, separate it into 6 equal pieces. Roll each piece into a ball and place them on the baking sheet, spaced apart. Cover with a clean kitchen towel or plastic wrap and let the dough rise again for 30 minutes, until puffed and airy.

Lightly flour the countertop with atta. Working with one dough ball at a time, roll it out with a rolling pin to an 8-inch-long (20 cm) oval. (It is okay if the dough is misshapen.) Repeat with each remaining dough ball, keeping the naans separate so they do not stick together, and cover with a clean kitchen towel so they do not dry out.

Heat a large cast-iron skillet or tawa over medium-high heat. Transfer a naan to the hot pan. It should cook quickly; flip it after 2 minutes or after it is lightly browned on the bottom and dry to the touch. Cook for 2 minutes on the other side, until lightly browned. Transfer the cooked naan to a plate and cover with a clean kitchen towel to keep warm. Repeat with the remaining naans.

When you're ready to serve, spread the garlic confit on the naans with a spoon. Sprinkle with cilantro and flaky salt and serve immediately.

Plain or garlic-topped naan can be wrapped in foil and stored in the freezer for up to 1 month. To reheat, bake from frozen, still wrapped in foil, at 350°F (175°C) for 10 minutes.

Green Onion (Scallion) Pancake

PYAAJ PARATHA

Paratha, a flaky flatbread, is delicious enough to eat on its own or with any curry and vegetables. Adding green onions to the paratha nods to Indian Chinese fusion, taking the techniques from Chinese scallion pancakes and combining them with the earthy taste of whole wheat paratha dough.

MAKES 8 PARATHAS; SERVES 4 TO 6

5 or 6 green onions (scallions)

2 batches Whole Wheat Flatbread dough (page 110), prepared through kneading

¼ cup (60 ml) vegetable oil

1 tablespoon flaky salt

Prepare the green onions by slicing off the roots. Thinly slice the green onions crosswise.

Divide the dough into 8 equal pieces. Lightly coat your hands with oil, then roll each piece into a ball about the size of a golf ball. Using a rolling pin, roll out a piece of dough to a circle about 6 inches (15 cm) across. Sprinkle 2 to 3 tablespoons of the green onions across the dough circle and lightly press them into the dough so they stick.

Roll the dough circle tightly into a cylinder, then coil the cylinder like a snail shell. Roll out the dough a second time to a circle 6 inches (15 cm) across. (It is okay if green onion pieces pierce through the dough.) Repeat with the remaining dough and green onions. Keep the parathas separate so they do not stick together, and cover with a clean kitchen towel so they do not dry out.

Heat a cast-iron skillet or tawa over medium-high heat and spread 1½ teaspoons oil across the pan. When the pan is hot and the oil is shiny, place a single paratha in the pan. Cook for 4 to 5 minutes on one side,

(continued)

letting the bottom get golden brown. Move it from time to time to ensure it's not sticking to the pan. Flip the paratha and cook for 4 to 5 minutes on the other side, until the paratha is golden brown and crispy. Wrap the cooked parathas in a clean kitchen towel to keep warm until you are ready to serve them. Repeat with the remaining parathas, making sure to re-oil the pan before placing each one in it. Top with flaky salt and serve warm.

Cooked parathas can be wrapped in foil and stored in the freezer for up to 1 month. To reheat, bake from frozen, still wrapped in foil, at 350°F (175°C) for 10 minutes.

Onion-Stuffed Flatbread

KULCHA

Kulchas (stuffed flatbreads) are even fluffier and chewier than naans. And thanks to their thickness, they are often filled with aromatics and served with chickpea curry and Pickled Onions (page 130). Make these kulchas ahead of time and store them in the freezer for a quick last-minute dinner or snack.

MAKES 6 KULCHAS

- **1 cup (240 ml) warm (110° to 115°F/43° to 46°C) water**
- **1 tablespoon granulated sugar**
- **1 packet (2¼ teaspoons/7 g) active dry yeast**
- **2½ cups (315 g) all-purpose flour**
- **2 tablespoons vegetable oil, plus more for rolling and greasing**
- **1 teaspoon table salt**
- **1 medium to large red or white onion, peeled**
- **2 teaspoons Garam Masala (page 146, or store-bought)**
- **1 tablespoon black sesame seeds, for topping**
- **Flaky salt, for topping**

Pour the water into a large mixing bowl or the bowl of a stand mixer. Sprinkle the sugar and yeast on top and stir to dissolve them. Wait 5 minutes for the yeast to bloom and bubble—it will look slightly puffed in appearance. If the yeast does not activate, start over with a new packet.

Add the all-purpose flour, oil, and table salt to the yeast mixture and stir with a spoon for 10 minutes, or fit the mixer with the dough hook attachment and mix for 8 minutes on medium speed. The dough should be supple and smooth. Transfer the ball of dough to a clean large mixing bowl and cover with plastic wrap or a clean kitchen towel. Set the bowl in a warm place and let the dough rise for 1 hour or until it is doubled in size.

(continued)

Lightly grease a baking sheet. Press the dough to release excess gas and separate the dough into 6 equal pieces. Roll each piece into a ball and place them on the baking sheet, spaced apart. Cover with a clean kitchen towel or plastic wrap and let the dough rise again for 30 minutes, until puffed and airy.

While the dough is on its second rise, mince the onion. Transfer the minced onion to a medium mixing bowl, add the garam masala, and toss to combine well.

Lightly oil the countertop and a rolling pin. Using the rolling pin, roll out each dough ball to a circle about 4 inches (10 cm) across **[1]**. Spoon 1 to 2 tablespoons of the spiced onions onto the middle of the circle **[2]**. Bring the edges of the dough together, pinching them into a ball **[3]**. Working with one ball of dough at a time, roll it out with the rolling pin to an 8-inch-long (20 cm) oval **[4]**. (It is okay if the dough is misshapen and onions are poking out.) Keep the kulchas separate so they do not stick together, and cover with a clean kitchen towel so they do not dry out.

Heat a large cast-iron skillet or tawa over medium-high heat for 2 to 3 minutes. Flick a few drops of water onto the pan—if they immediately sizzle and evaporate, the pan is ready. Transfer a kulcha to the hot pan. The kulcha should cook quickly for just 2 minutes, until lightly browned on the bottom and dry to the touch. Flip the kulcha and cook for 2 minutes on the other side, until lightly browned. Transfer the kulcha to a plate and cover with a clean kitchen towel to keep warm. Repeat with the remaining kulchas.

Top the kulchas with sesame seeds and flaky salt and serve while still hot.

NOTE: *You can make the kulcha dough in advance and freeze it after shaping it into ovals. To freeze, stack the kulchas with parchment paper between them to prevent sticking, then place in a resealable bag. Store in the freezer for up to 1 month. Transfer a frozen kulcha to a hot pan, cooking it for an extra 2 to 3 minutes per side.*

1

2

3

4

The Anatomy of a Thali

Indians love to present a spectrum of textures, flavors, and temperatures within a single meal. Enter the thali, literally meaning "plate," decorated with curries, crispy bits, dry sabzis, pickles, and sweets. Thalis are enjoyed casually in canteens for a weekday lunch, or elaborately adorned and served at weddings. Across India, they are prepared with endless variations, depending on the specialties of the region. Creamy daal makhani (buttery lentils) and naan (bread) dot Punjabi plates; thick vegetable stews and coconut rice decorate South Indian thalis.

The most classic thalis look like large stainless-steel plates with an arrangement of steel bowls. The base of a thali is usually a large, round plate with partitions or bowls to hold curries, soups, and vegetables. The sauciest curries live in small, deep bowls clustered on one edge of the thali. Next to them, directly on the plate, are dry-roasted or grilled vegetables and sabzis. Heaped mounds of rice sit on another edge of the plate, covered with a freshly cooked roti (flatbread). In the midst of the curries and sabzis are small bowls of pickles and yogurt.

A well-balanced thali satisfies the main flavors your tongue tastes: sweetness, umami, bitterness, sourness, and saltiness. Make sure to incorporate both spicy and cooling elements, such as plant-based yogurt, into each spread to help relieve the palate in between bites. Aside from the core flavors, textures play a key part of a delicious thali. Crunchy pickled onions and ginger dot the inner gaps between the small bowls of savory dishes and the soft, chewy piles of rice. Flaky, buttery flatbreads are there to scoop up tender vegetable dishes.

Salt is a no-brainer for any savory dish, but in Indian food, it plays the critical role of suppressing the bitterness of vegetable dishes and balancing pungent spices like cumin and cardamom. Indian recipes introduce sweetness through natural ingredients like jaggery, coconut milk, dates, caramelized onions—even yams. Sweetness provides a

(continued)

much-welcome contrast to the heat and saltiness in most savory dishes. Umami arrives on thalis via tomatoes, dried mango powder, cumin, and fermented lentils. These ingredients bounce off the saltiness and paint the palate with complex, savory flavor profiles. Radishes, Green Chutney (page 134), and garlic add a fresh bitterness needed to offset sweet and sour elements on the plate. Sourness, one of the most common flavors in Indian dishes, shines through squeezes of lemon, blended tamarind pastes, and raw mango. These tart elements balance the otherwise rich ingredients and spices. Sour ingredients also help balance the saltiness of a food—a quick way to remedy an oversalted daal is to add a squeeze of lemon juice. Spiciness, the most common flavor associated with Indian food, heightens the earthiness of umami and makes a dish more savory. Instead of adding spice via a single ingredient, Indian cooking calls for a variety of steps that delicately impart heat and spice to a recipe. Dried red chilis add a smoky taste, while fresh green chiles are used to add an earthy, citrusy spice. Finally, cooling elements like fresh cucumber and plant-based yogurt provide relief between bites of every deeply seasoned curry and sabzi.

Get creative with your pairings when making your own arrangement of a thali. You can make a breakfast-themed thali, or highlight all the produce of the season in one platter. Always serve rice in a thali to provide a neutral vehicle to carry any curries and chutneys. Remember, your thali does not have to follow a strict set of rules. To build your thali, think of dishes that highlight each of the flavors and vary in texture. Some ideas for combinations:

	THALI 1	THALI 2	THALI 3
SALTY	Stuffed Okra and Eggplant (page 69)	Spinach with Whole Roasted Cauliflower (page 83)	Tofu Tikka (page 75)
SOUR	Rasam Cabbage Rolls (page 71)	Cracked Wheat with Poached Rhubarb (page 31)	Braised Spring Pea–Semolina Porridge (page 33)
SPICY	Pickled Ginger and Chiles (page 131)	Spiced Potato Sandwiches with Jalapeño Chutney (page 25)	Massaman Lentil Curry (page 77)
UMAMI	Go-To Lentil Curry (page 88)	All-Day Chickpea Curry (page 80)	Tomato Chutney (page 137)
BITTER	Garlic and Leek Lentil Fritters (page 39)	Corn with Puffed Rice (page 54)	Pomegranate-Radish Salad (page 129)
COOLING	Heirloom Tomato and Fruit Chaat (page 57)	Pickled Onions (page 130)	Tomato and Cucumber Salad (page 145)
SWEET	Flaky Butternut Squash Flatbread (page 23)	Brussels Sprouts Manchurian (page 91)	Masala Yams with Ramp Chimichurri (page 59)

Sauces & Sides

The sauces and pickle-y sides dotting every Indian spread are just as critical to the meal as the curries, biryanis, and parathas. Balance warm and spicy curries with palate-cooling quick pickles, salads, and chutneys.

Pomegranate-Radish Salad

MOOLI KA LACHHA

Mooli ka lachha (grated daikon salad) adds a tangy and sharp kick when you are begging for a fresh bite. The pomegranate brings sweetness that is the tart foil to the roasted potatoes in Potato Patties with Pomegranate-Radish Salad (page 63) or with Massaman Lentil Curry (page 77). Kala namak adds an extra layer of umami that is reminiscent of MSG. Try experimenting with purple daikon or watermelon radishes for a vibrant salad topping.

SERVES 8

1 pomegranate

1 medium to large daikon radish (about 14 ounces/400 g), trimmed and peeled

2 serrano chiles, stems removed

½ teaspoon kala namak (black salt)

½ teaspoon table salt

Juice of 1 lemon

Seed the pomegranate by slicing it into quarters, then pulling back the corners of each piece to naturally loosen the seeds. Put the arils in a large mixing bowl. Grate the daikon on the largest holes of a box grater and add it to the pomegranate arils. Cut the chiles crosswise into thin slices and add them to the bowl. Add the black salt, table salt, and lemon juice and mix everything thoroughly. Allow the salad to sit for 30 minutes before serving or using as a topping.

Store in an airtight container for up to 5 days in the fridge. The flavors will intensify over time.

Pickled Onions

Indian quick-pickled onions are one of the most useful condiments. They successfully cool your palate and add crunch to a dish, and it takes no time to make a new batch every week. Pair them with daal or beans or add as a topping for Masala Yams with Ramp Chimichurri (page 59).

MAKES ABOUT 1½ CUPS (360 ML); SERVES 4

1 large red onion, peeled
Juice of 1 lemon
1 teaspoon granulated sugar
1 teaspoon table salt

Cut the onion in half lengthwise, then slice each half into thin half-moons. Put the onion slices in a clean glass jar. Pour the lemon juice over the onions. Add the sugar and salt and cap the jar tightly before shaking it to mix everything together. Check to make sure the sugar and salt dissolve completely in the lemon juice. Serve the onions right away, or place in the fridge to cure for about an hour.

Store pickled onions in the fridge for up to 1 week. They will become softer over time.

Pickled Ginger and Chiles

If green chiles are too spicy for your taste, the ginger tastes delicious pickled on its own, and imparts accompanying dishes with a slight edge. Try these pickles with Masala Yams with Ramp Chimichurri (page 59) or Chile "Cheese" Lentil Pancakes (page 17).

MAKES ABOUT 1½ CUPS (360 ML); SERVES 6 TO 8

2 pieces fresh ginger (4 to 5 inches/10 to 12.5 cm each), peeled

6 jalapeño chiles, stems removed

Juice of 3 lemons, strained

1½ teaspoons table salt

Prepare the ginger by first slicing it lengthwise into ¼-inch-thick (6 mm) slices. Stack a few at a time and cut into thin matchsticks. Transfer the ginger to a clean 12-ounce (360 ml) glass jar.

Slice the jalapeños crosswise into ¼-inch-thick (6 mm) rounds and add them to the ginger. Pour in the lemon juice; it should cover the ginger and chiles completely. If it doesn't, add more freshly squeezed lemon juice.

Add the salt and close the jar tightly. Shake vigorously to mix everything together. Let the pickle sit in the fridge for 2 to 3 days before serving so that the ginger can fully absorb the acid and soften.

The pickled ginger and chiles can last in the fridge for up to 3 weeks.

How to Pickle Anything

My go-to pickles are onion and ginger, but my great aunts and grandmothers are known to pickle anything under the sun. Unlike the long-form hot-pickling methods used for dill pickles, the Indian method requires no heat, no vinegar, and not much time at all. Instead, Indian quick pickles use lemon juice for preservation and an added fruity flavor. Most humble vegetables you can find year-round will make a delicious pickle. Raw cauliflower, green mango, radish slices, and spring peas all thrive in a sour setting, and taste even better the longer they get to swim in their lemony pickling liquid. Pickles are delicious whether enjoyed alone as a snack with fresh bread or with rich stews like Go-To Lentil Curry (page 88).

To quick-pickle, add enough freshly squeezed lemon juice to completely cover bite-size pieces of vegetables in a glass jar. Add 1 teaspoon table salt for every 6 tablespoons (90 ml) juice you add. For a subtly warm and spicy undertone, throw in chopped green chiles according to your spice tolerance. For starchier, harder vegetables like carrots or cauliflower florets, let the pickle sit in the fridge for a day or two to help the vegetables soften before eating. A general rule to follow is if you are comfortable eating the vegetable raw, pickle it!

Green Chutney

More often than not, the green sauce served at any Indian restaurant is some variation of a mint and cilantro chutney. Traditionally, this chutney is made by blending all the ingredients raw. But shocking the herbs in boiling water followed by an ice bath will help preserve the chutney's vibrant green color and keep the chutney's flavor fresh for longer.

MAKES ABOUT 1 CUP (200 G)

1 bunch cilantro (about 2 ounces/ 50 g), rinsed

1 bunch mint (about 2 ounces/50 g), leaves only

3 garlic cloves, peeled

1-inch (2.5 cm) piece fresh ginger, peeled and chopped

Juice of 1 lemon

1 fresh green chile pepper, stem removed, chopped

½ teaspoon table salt

½ teaspoon granulated sugar

Bring a pot of water to a boil. Prepare an ice bath by filling a large bowl with equal parts cold water and ice cubes. Lay out a clean kitchen towel or several layers of paper towels, for drying the blanched herbs.

Chop off and discard the last ½-inch (1 cm) of the cilantro stems. Add the cilantro and mint leaves to the boiling water for 1 minute. Use a spider or slotted spoon to transfer the herbs to the ice bath. Submerge them for 1 minute, until cold, before placing them on the kitchen towel to dry.

Put the blanched herbs, garlic, and ginger in a blender. Add the lemon juice, green chile, salt, and sugar. Blend until the chutney is smooth, with no chunks or herb leaves remaining. The consistency should resemble chimichurri. Serve the chutney immediately alongside your dishes.

Store leftover chutney in an airtight container in the fridge for up to 1 week.

Red Chutney

Tamarind, known as imli in Hindi, is a sweet and sour tropical fruit that often shows up as a tangy yet molasses-y chutney. Following the tamarind, jaggery—an unrefined palm sugar with deep caramel flavors—is the costar in this chutney. If you are unable to find jaggery, feel free to substitute an equal amount of dark brown sugar. This versatile chutney will taste great drizzled on top of a bowl of chickpeas as well as roasted vegetables.

MAKES 2 CUPS (480 ML)

1 teaspoon vegetable oil
1 teaspoon cumin seeds
½ teaspoon red chili powder
½ teaspoon ground coriander
1 cup (190 g) jaggery or loosely packed dark brown sugar
½ cup (120 ml) tamarind concentrate
2 cups (480 ml) water
½ teaspoon table salt

Begin by blooming your spices: Heat the oil in a medium pot over medium-low heat. Once the oil is warm and shimmering, about 1 minute, add the cumin seeds, red chili powder, and coriander. Continuously stir the spices until fragrant and toasted, about 1 minute.

Pour the jaggery, tamarind concentrate, water, and salt into the pot with the spices and stir to combine. Bring the mixture to a hard simmer, when the sauce bubbles around the perimeter of the pot, then reduce the heat to low. Cook the chutney for 5 to 7 minutes, stirring occasionally so it doesn't burn on the bottom. Some of the water will evaporate as the chutney thickens into a smooth, gravy-like sauce. The chutney is done when it easily coats the back of a spoon. Let the chutney cool before serving.

Store extra tamarind chutney in an airtight container in the fridge for up to 1 week.

NOTE: *Tamarind concentrate, which is stocked in the canned food or international aisle, is sometimes difficult to find. Look for dried seedless tamarind instead. You can soak ½ cup (120 g) dried tamarind overnight in water, drain it, then blend with 2 tablespoons water to make your own concentrate.*

Tomato Chutney

South Indian savories are not complete without a side of tomato chutney. Typically this chutney is blended and cooked for a long time, but this version preserves tomatoes' freshness by adding them last. You can use the same amount of any tomato here, but opting for whole cherry tomatoes will play up the subtle sweetness that makes this chutney as delectable as can be. Dip Flaky Butternut Squash Flatbread (page 23) in it, or serve it alongside biryani or even crepes.

MAKES 2 CUPS (250 G)

6 garlic cloves, peeled

2-inch (5 cm) piece fresh ginger, peeled

2 cups (290 g) cherry or grape tomatoes

¼ cup (60 ml) extra virgin olive oil

1 teaspoon black mustard seeds

½ teaspoon cumin seeds

2 dried red chilis

1 teaspoon granulated sugar

½ teaspoon table salt

Slice the garlic lengthwise into long, thin chips. Slice the ginger into ⅛-inch-thick (3 mm) matchsticks. Make a small slit lengthwise in each tomato. (This will help the tomatoes burst and cook quickly later on.)

Pour the olive oil into a stainless-steel or cast-iron skillet and set it over medium-low heat. Once the oil is glossy and coats the pan easily, about 3 minutes, add the mustard seeds, cumin seeds, and dried chilis. Toast the spices for 1 to 2 minutes, until they are sizzling and crackling.

Add the garlic and ginger to the oil and cook for 2 to 3 minutes, until they soften and smell noticeably fragrant. Add the tomatoes along with the sugar and salt. Cook for 10 to 15 minutes over medium-low heat, stirring occasionally. The tomatoes will burst and release their liquid. By halfway through cooking, after 5 to 7 minutes, the water in the tomatoes will start evaporating as they break down into a saucy consistency. Keep cooking the tomatoes until the excess liquid is cooked off and the tomatoes are soft and jammy. The more moisture you cook off from the tomatoes, the thicker the chutney will be.

(continued)

Transfer the chutney to a glass jar or container and allow it to cool completely, uncovered. Serve at room temperature.

Store in the fridge, tightly covered, for up to 1 week.

Freestyle It

- This chutney tastes great with more garlic or ginger, so add more according to your taste. Feel free to add up to 1 cup (135 g) sliced garlic—from about 2 medium bulbs—for a more pungent chutney.

Spicy Ketchup

Spicy ketchup will add a warm kick and a bit of sweetness to any snack you'd normally have with ketchup.

MAKES 1 CUP (240 G)

2 tablespoons Garam Masala (page 146, or store-bought)

1 tablespoon cayenne pepper

1 cup (235 g) ketchup

Heat a medium nonstick skillet or saucepan over medium heat. Add the garam masala and cayenne and toast for about 3 minutes, until the spices have darkened and are fragrant. Add the ketchup. Using a spatula, combine the ketchup and spices thoroughly. Remove the pan from the heat and allow the ketchup to fully cool before serving.

Transfer to an airtight jar and store in the fridge for up to 1 month.

Masala Cashew Cream

The key to making creamy, tikka-style sauces is not dairy, but cashews. Indians have used cashews to thicken their sauces and curries for centuries—their fat content and creamy, neutral base mimic the texture and taste of heavy cream. Masala cashew cream can be used in any dish in place of coconut milk or heavy cream; mix it into a dish that has too much acidity or spice to mellow it out. This base can be used in Tofu Tikka (page 75) and Spinach with Whole Roasted Cauliflower (page 83), as well as soups and stews.

MAKES 3 CUPS (600 G)

1 cup (120 g) raw, unsalted cashews

3 cups (720 ml) boiling water

1 medium red or white onion, peeled

6 garlic cloves, peeled

2-inch (5 cm) piece fresh ginger, peeled

2 medium Roma tomatoes

1 tablespoon vegetable oil

1 teaspoon table salt

1 teaspoon Garam Masala (page 146, or store-bought)

½ teaspoon red chili powder

1 tablespoon water

Combine the cashews and boiling water in a large mixing bowl. Loosely cover with a clean kitchen towel and set aside to soak for at least 30 minutes and up to 2 hours.

Finely mince the onions, garlic, and ginger. Chop the tomatoes into ¼-inch (6 mm) cubes.

Pour the oil into a Dutch oven or large, heavy-bottomed saucepan and set it over medium heat. Once the oil is glistening, after about 2 minutes, add the salt, tomatoes, and onions. Cook, stirring constantly, until the tomatoes begin to break down and lose their water and the onions are translucent, 5 to 7 minutes. The tomato-onion mixture will appear chunky and pasty. Add the garlic and ginger, garam masala, and red chili powder and stir, combining them thoroughly with the vegetables. Cook for 1 to 2 minutes, until the garlic and ginger are soft and fragrant.

Drain the cashews in a colander or fine-mesh sieve. Put them in a blender along with the contents of the pan and 1 tablespoon water. Blend into a smooth paste. If the paste still looks granular after blending for 2 to 3 minutes, add more water, 1½ teaspoons at a time, until the mixture is creamy.

Pour the sauce back into the pan and cook for a few more minutes, until it has darkened and thickened slightly. Use immediately, or store in an airtight container in the fridge for up to 5 days.

Chili Oil

CHHONK

Many cultures have their own version of chili oils or chili crisps, and chhonk (also known as tadka) is the Indian version. Indian families often own small cast-iron pans dedicated solely to making chhonk. While chhonk is traditionally made with ghee, here the peppery notes of olive oil distinctly complement the spices and make this chhonk fully vegan. Chhonk is traditionally used to top daals, yogurt rice, and curries, but you can use it on dips like hummus or anywhere else you like to use a chili crisp.

MAKES 1 CUP (240 ML)

½ cup (120 ml) olive oil

10 to 12 fresh curry leaves, stems removed and discarded

1 teaspoon black mustard seeds

1 teaspoon cumin seeds

1 teaspoon black peppercorns

1 teaspoon table salt

5 or 6 dried red chilis

Pour the olive oil into a small cast-iron or stainless-steel skillet and set over medium heat. Allow the oil to heat for 3 to 4 minutes, until the oil is glistening. Add a couple of mustard seeds to the oil; if they immediately rise to the surface and bubble, the oil is ready.

Add the curry leaves, mustard seeds, cumin seeds, peppercorns, salt, and dried chilis to the oil. Fry the spices for 3 to 4 minutes, until you can smell their aromas and hear them crackling. Use a wooden or silicone spoon or spatula to continuously swirl the spices and oil to cook them evenly. Keep an eye on them to ensure they are fried but not burnt; the curry leaves will become crispy and lightly brown. Remove the pan from heat and transfer the chhonk into a heatproof bowl.

Use it to top any dish you like.

Store chhonk in an airtight container in a cool, dry place for up to 1 week.

(continued)

Freestyle It

- If you can't find curry leaves, feel free to grab sage from the herb section and use it in their place. While the flavor will be completely different, sage's leaf structure holds up in the oil and will perfume the chhonk while frying to a crisp, just like curry leaves would.
- Play with the spices as well. If you crave an autumnal, warm fragrance from your chhonk, add cinnamon sticks, cardamom pods, and whole cloves. If you want an aromatic, pungent chhonk, use a mix of fresh green chiles and dried red ones (5 to 6 total), minced ginger, and shallots. If you are missing one of the spices in the original recipe, feel free to omit it or use the ground version.

Tomato and Cucumber Salad

Also sometimes called kachumber, tomato and cucumber salad is a common opener to North Indian meals. You will find it among the plates of curries and sabzis as a raw bite of freshness to accompany rich and spicy dishes. The kala namak draws out the juices from the tomatoes and cucumbers while imparting a hint of funky umami to them.

SERVES 4

2 English or slicing cucumbers (about 7 ounces/200 g total)

2 large beefsteak or heirloom tomatoes

Juice of ½ lemon

1 teaspoon flaky salt

½ teaspoon kala namak (black salt)

Peel the cucumbers using a vegetable peeler. Slice the cucumbers and tomatoes into ¼-inch-thick (6 mm) rounds. Arrange the slices on a plate. Sprinkle the lemon juice evenly over the salad. Sprinkle on the flaky salt and kala namak. Serve immediately for the freshest taste.

Garam Masala

You can find every Indian spice mix at the grocery store, but the one worth making from scratch is garam masala. Store-bought garam masala does not compare to the intensely warm and customizable fragrance of your own homemade masala. Making your own spice mix is a labor of love. Use it to enhance salad dressings, roasted veggies, or curries.

MAKES 1 CUP (125 G)

¼ cup (30 g) coriander seeds

2 tablespoons green cardamom pods

2 tablespoons cumin seeds

1 tablespoon black peppercorns

1 tablespoon whole cloves

4 dried bay leaves

2 cinnamon sticks

2 star anise pods

First toast the spices to warm their natural oils and enhance their fragrances: Place the coriander, cardamom, cumin, peppercorns, cloves, bay leaves, cinnamon, and star anise in a small nonstick or cast-iron skillet and set it over low heat. Using a spatula, move the spices around the pan constantly to ensure even toasting. The spices should begin to emit a warm aroma as they roast. Toast the spices for 3 to 4 minutes total, ensuring they do not burn. Once the spices are toasted, transfer them to a rimmed baking sheet and spread them out evenly to cool.

Once fully cooled, transfer the spices to a spice grinder or food processor. Grind until the mixture is coarse, similar to the texture of granulated sugar. Depending on the size of your grinder or blender, you may need to grind the garam masala in batches. Transfer the garam masala to a glass jar and seal tightly.

Store garam masala in a cool, dry place for 10 months to 1 year.

Sweets & Treats

Desserts in a culture where ovens were not historically present can undoubtedly get creative. Indian desserts take the form of chilled rice puddings, custards, and even snow cones. Warming spices, tropical fruits, and lots of nuts shine in these not-too-sweet, sometimes spicy desserts.

Strained Yogurt with Apricot-Cardamom Compote

SHRIKHAND

Shrikhand, a custardy, thick yogurt dessert, takes little to no effort to make—simply strain plant-based yogurt overnight, then top it with a quick, jammy apricot-cardamom compote. Cardamom and sugar perfume the otherwise tangy yogurt with an autumnal, classically Indian fragrance. Coconut-based yogurt works best for this dish, as the coconut flavor complements the apricots well, and tastes especially good in the summer.

SERVES 6

SHRIKHAND

3 cups (720 g) unsweetened plant-based yogurt

Seeds from 1 tablespoon green cardamom pods

½ cup (100 g) granulated sugar

COMPOTE

4 fresh apricots (see Note)

¼ cup (55 g) packed brown sugar

Juice of ½ lemon

1 cinnamon stick

1 tablespoon green cardamom pods

Place a double layer of cheesecloth in a fine-mesh sieve suspended over a large, deep mixing bowl, leaving plenty of distance between the bottom of the sieve and the bowl. Pour the yogurt into the cheesecloth. Cover the sieve and bowl with a clean kitchen towel and let the yogurt drain in the fridge overnight.

Discard the drained whey, dry the bowl, and transfer the yogurt back to the bowl. The yogurt will be much denser, almost as thick as butter. Coarsely chop the cardamom seeds and add them, along with the granulated sugar, to the yogurt. Whisk thoroughly. Refrigerate until you're ready to serve.

(continued)

Slice the apricots in half and discard the pits. Place them in a small saucepan with the brown sugar, lemon juice, cinnamon stick, and cardamom pods. Cook over medium heat for 10 to 12 minutes, stirring constantly. The apricots should break down and become jam-like in texture, while the sugar fully dissolves. Remove the apricots from the heat and discard the cinnamon stick and cardamom pods. Let cool to room temperature, or chill in the fridge.

Spoon the shrikhand into serving bowls and top with the apricot compote. Chill to serve cold, or serve at room temperature.

Store the shrikhand and apricot compote separately in the fridge for up to 5 days.

NOTE: *When fresh apricots are out of season, you can use an equal amount of any other stone fruit or berries.*

Roasted Strawberry–Almond Milk Rice Pudding

KHEER

Indian rice pudding, or kheer, can be served hot or cold, and infused or topped with your favorite fruits and nuts. Roasting the strawberries will release their sugars and caramelize them, adding more complexity than fresh fruit does. Feel free to include pistachios, almond slivers, and raisins in the kheer while it is cooking. If you do not have strawberries, substitute any stone fruit or berry in season.

SERVES 4 TO 6

1 cup (180 g) basmati rice

2 cups (290 g) strawberries

1 cup (200 g) granulated sugar

Table salt

1½ teaspoons green cardamom pods

2 tablespoons (30 g) plant-based butter

¼ cup (30 g) raw, unsalted cashews

4 cups (1 L) unsweetened almond milk

Preheat the oven to 350°F (175°C). Line a baking sheet with parchment paper. Place the rice in a fine-mesh sieve and rinse under cold water until the water runs clear, using your hands to stir and move the rice around to wash away more starch. Drain well and set aside.

Slice the stems off the strawberries and cut them in half lengthwise. Transfer the strawberries to the lined baking sheet and sprinkle with ¼ cup (50 g) of the sugar and a pinch of salt. Toss the strawberries in the sugar so they are evenly coated. Roast in the oven for 15 minutes, until they are tender and slightly browned. Set the roasted strawberries aside.

(continued)

Using the broad, flat side of a large knife, smash the cardamom pods so they split open. Heat a Dutch oven or heavy-bottomed pot over medium heat. Add the butter, cardamom seeds, rice, and cashews. Mix the spices, rice, and nuts so they are evenly coated with butter. (The goal is to toast the ingredients and impart their fragrances to the butter.) Continuously stir so the rice and nuts do not burn; cook for 4 minutes or until they take on a slightly toasted color.

Add the almond milk, the remaining ¾ cup (150 g) sugar, and another pinch of salt. Stir everything so the rice is fully submerged in the milk. Bring the milk to a hard simmer, with small bubbles continuously rising to the surface. Reduce the heat to low and cook the rice for 10 to 15 minutes. Stir every 2 to 3 minutes to prevent the rice from sticking to the bottom of the pot. At the 10 minute mark, taste a grain of rice to ensure it is fully cooked; it should be soft and fluffy. Once the kheer has a porridge-like consistency, remove the pot from the heat.

Divide the kheer into serving bowls and top with the roasted strawberries. Enjoy hot or at room temperature.

Store kheer in the fridge in a covered container for up to 3 days; serve cold.

Freestyle It

› Kheer is a sweet porridge ready to take on any grain. Semolina, broken vermicelli noodles, and dalia (cracked wheat) are common alternatives. But you can get creative: Use oats. Try quinoa. Make sure to toast any grain in butter just as you would the rice. When it comes to liquids, use 4 cups (1 L) of plant-based milk for every 1 cup (180 g) of hearty grain. But ultimately, the consistency is up to your preference.

Black Forest Cake

Though Black Forest cake is originally German, South Asians have been putting their own twist on it for decades. Because many desserts in India are eggless, this is a less rich version than its namesake. Fluffy whipped coconut cream and an oil-based cake create an airy and light dessert that is commonly served at Indian birthday celebrations; the addition of cherries adds a slight tartness to cut through the sweet chocolate cake layers.

SERVES 6 TO 8

CAKE

- 1 tablespoon (15 g) plant-based butter
- 3 cups (375 g) all-purpose flour
- 2 cups (400 g) granulated sugar
- ½ cup (45 g) cocoa powder
- 2 teaspoons baking soda
- 1 teaspoon table salt
- 2 cups (480 ml) lukewarm water
- 1 tablespoon instant coffee powder
- ¾ cup (180 g) vegetable oil
- 2 tablespoons freshly squeezed lemon juice or apple cider vinegar

ASSEMBLY AND FROSTING

- 2 cans (27 ounces/800 ml) coconut cream
- 1 cup (110 g) confectioners' sugar
- ½ cup (120 g) cherry jam
- ½ cup (55 g) pitted fresh sweet cherries, preferably with stems, for garnish
- ½ cup (65 g) grated semisweet chocolate, for garnish

Preheat the oven to 350°F (175°C). Grease two 8-inch (20 cm) round cake pans with the butter.

Mix the flour, granulated sugar, cocoa powder, baking soda, and salt in a large mixing bowl with a whisk. Combine the water and coffee powder in a small bowl until the coffee is fully dissolved. Pour the coffee into the dry ingredients. Add the vegetable oil and lemon juice to the batter and whisk thoroughly for 1 minute. The batter will be thin and ribbony.

(continued)

Pour the batter into the two prepared pans and place on the center rack in the oven. Bake for 25 minutes. To check if the cake is fully baked, insert a toothpick or fork into the cake. If it comes out clean, the cake is ready. If the cake is underbaked and there is wet batter on the tester, continue to bake it, and test its readiness again every 5 minutes.

Remove the pans from the oven and allow them to cool for 10 minutes. Turn out the cake layers onto a wire rack and let them cool fully for at least 30 minutes.

To prepare the frosting, place the coconut cream and confectioners' sugar in the bowl of a stand mixer or a large mixing bowl. Fit the stand mixer with the whisk attachment or use an electric hand mixer and beat the cream and sugar on medium speed for 4 to 5 minutes, until the cream is fluffy and the sugar is fully incorporated. The texture should be similar to whipped cream, creating stiff peaks when you scoop some up.

Assemble the cake. If the cake layers are not flat on top, use a serrated knife to slice off a thin layer from the top to even them out. Place one layer on a plate as the base and top it with the cherry jam and a few tablespoons of whipped cream. Evenly spread the jam and cream on the layer. Place the second layer on top. Start by dolloping about ½ cup (60 g) of the whipped cream frosting on top of the cake. Use an offset spatula to distribute the frosting and spread it out in circular motions. Continue to add frosting and spread it down the sides of the cake until the cake is evenly covered. Top the cake with the whole cherries and chocolate shavings. Slice and serve.

NOTE: *The cake can be baked and frosted 1 day in advance and stored, loosely covered, in the fridge. Allow it to come to room temperature for 1 hour before garnishing and serving.*

Freestyle It

- If you don't have round cake pans, you can bake this cake in a 13 × 9-inch (33 × 23 cm) baking pan. The baking time will be closer to 20 minutes. Slice the cake in half crosswise and stack the rectangles on top of each other when assembling, filling and frosting them the same way.

Jaggery Semolina Pudding

SOOJI HALWA

South Asians have the unique ability to turn any grain—and even some vegetables—into halwa, a dry, dense, and soft porridge. Sooji (semolina) is a classic version thanks to how quickly it absorbs and complements the deep caramelized flavors of sugar and butter. This recipe calls for jaggery to emulate that nutty, earthy flavor you'd normally taste from the ghee in halwa, but feel free to opt for dark brown sugar if you cannot find it.

SERVES 4 TO 6

½ cup (1 stick/115 to 125 g) plant-based butter

½ cup (90 g) sooji (whole semolina grains)

2 tablespoons whole raw cashews

½ cup (95 g) jaggery or loosely packed dark brown sugar

½ cup (120 ml) plant-based milk of your choice

½ cup (120 ml) water

2 tablespoons golden raisins

Pinch of table salt

Melt the butter in a deep nonstick skillet over medium-low heat. Add the semolina and cashews and mix with a spatula, coating everything with the melted butter. Continue to stir the semolina and cashews to lightly roast them, 4 to 5 minutes; the semolina should be light brown. Mix at least every 2 minutes, and be careful to not burn the semolina.

After the sooji is toasted, add the jaggery, milk, water, golden raisins, and salt. Stir together until the mixture resembles a grainy pudding. Continue to stir the sooji as it absorbs the milk and water, about 5 minutes. The halwa is done when the semolina granules are clumping together, resembling a dense porridge. Divide the halwa into bowls and serve hot, at room temperature, or cold.

Store in the fridge for up to 3 days. To reheat, sprinkle a little water on the halwa and microwave for 2 minutes.

Rose-Pistachio Rice Noodles

FALOODA

Rice noodles seem like an uncommon dessert ingredient, but when soaked in rose syrup and creamy oat milk, they turn into a slurpable pudding. Rooh afza (rose syrup) can be found in Indian and Middle Eastern stores, and is a versatile ingredient to keep in the pantry to top ice cream and kheer (page 153).

SERVES 4

1 cup (165 g) chia seeds

1 cup (237 ml) oat milk

5 ounces (150 g) thin rice vermicelli noodles

½ cup (65 g) shelled unsalted pistachios, chopped

2 tablespoons rooh afza (rose syrup)

Plant-based vanilla ice cream, for serving

Combine the chia seeds in a medium bowl with the oat milk and mix fully, so no clumps remain. Set aside at room temperature or in the fridge for at least 2 hours. After soaking, the chia seeds should be gelatinous and doubled in volume.

Bring a large pot of water to a boil over high heat. Cook the vermicelli according to the instructions on the package. Drain the cooked noodles in a fine-mesh sieve and rinse under cold water to stop the cooking. Combine the noodles with the rooh afza until they are fully coated.

Scoop vanilla ice cream into dessert coupes. Layer enough vermicelli noodles to cover the ice cream. Top with an equal portion of the chia seed mixture and sprinkle with pistachios. Serve immediately to prevent the noodles from becoming soggy.

Tamarind Snow Cone

ICE GOLA

Ice golas are Indian snow cones—gola literally translates to "ball." They can be served with a variety of syrups; this recipe transforms Red Chutney (page 136) into a spicy caramel sauce to drizzle on top. In a pinch, look for tamarind chutney in the pantry section of your local Indian store. Enjoy this quick recipe on a hot summer day.

SERVES 4

½ cup (75 g) Red Chutney (page 136)

½ cup (100 g) granulated sugar

½ cup (120 ml) water

4 cups (1 L) ice cubes

1 teaspoon kala namak (black salt), for garnish

First, make the syrup. Combine the chutney, sugar, and water in a small saucepan and set it over medium heat. Bring to a simmer while stirring constantly with a spatula so the sugar fully dissolves and the chutney is well incorporated. Reduce the heat to low and simmer the syrup for 5 minutes, stirring continuously to prevent it from burning onto the bottom of the pan, until it has thickened enough to coat the back of a spoon. Transfer the syrup to a glass jar and put in the fridge for 1 to 2 hours to cool completely.

Pulse the ice in a food processor or blender until it forms an icy powder, like a snow cone. Transfer the shaved ice into four bowls. Top each bowl with a few spoons of tamarind syrup and a pinch of black salt and serve at once.

Fruit Cream

Shout-out to all the Indian moms who use the oven for storage rather than baking and therefore make fruit cream their go-to dessert instead. This vegan custard tastes rich without the addition of eggs but with the right proportions of cornstarch and coconut milk. Top the extra-creamy dessert with fresh berries and tart orange pieces.

SERVES 8

- 4 cups (1 L) plant-based milk of your choice
- 1 teaspoon pure vanilla extract
- Pinch of table salt
- 1 cup (200 g) granulated sugar
- ½ cup (65 g) cornstarch
- ½ cup (120 ml) full-fat coconut milk
- 4 tablespoons (½ stick/60 g) unsalted plant-based butter
- ½ cup (75 g) seedless grapes
- ½ cup (75 g) fresh strawberries, stems removed
- 1 banana
- 1 orange
- ½ cup (75 g) fresh blueberries
- ½ cup (70 g) fresh blackberries

Bring the plant-based milk, vanilla, and salt to a boil in a Dutch oven or heavy-bottomed pot over medium heat.

While the plant-based milk heats, mix together the sugar, cornstarch, and coconut milk in a large mixing bowl. Use a whisk to fully combine everything, ensuring no lumps of sugar or cornstarch remain.

Once the plant-based milk is boiling, reduce the heat to medium-low. Using a silicone spatula, stir the sugar-cornstarch into the plant-based milk. Whisk vigorously to combine for 3 minutes, and continue whisking until the mixture feels heavy against the whisk. (If you stop whisking, you run the risk of overcooking parts of the cream into lumps.) The mixture should thicken and resemble pudding.

(continued)

Transfer the cooked cream to a clean heatproof mixing bowl and add the butter 1 tablespoon at a time. With each addition, whisk until the butter is fully incorporated. Repeat until you've added all the butter. You should have a smooth, custard-like cream. If it has lumps, strain it through a fine-mesh sieve into a clean bowl. Cover the cream with plastic wrap so the wrap is touching the surface, and chill in the fridge for at least 2 hours.

Prepare the fruit. Slice the grapes and strawberries in half. Peel the banana and slice it into coins. Peel the orange and cut it across the grain into thin, round slices. Mix the grapes, strawberries, banana, orange, blueberries, and blackberries in a bowl.

Remove the cold cream from the fridge and whisk to break it up. Add three-quarters of the fruit to the cream, reserving the rest for topping. Mix the cream and fruit gently but thoroughly with a spatula. Divide the fruit cream into serving bowls and top with the remaining fruit. Serve cold.

Store Fruit Cream in the fridge in an airtight container for up to 3 days. Do not be alarmed if the cut fruit browns slightly; the taste will remain the same.

Mixed Nuts and Dates Roll

BURFI

These fudge-like Indian sweets can be made from cooking down dates, nuts, and even squash into compact, richly flavored bites. This burfi is sweetened only with softened dates; it has no added sugar and requires no baking, making it an easy and healthy dessert option. Though the recipe calls for pistachios, cashews, and walnuts, feel free to use a single nut or a mixture of any unsalted nuts you have on hand.

SERVES 8

2 cups (250 g) whole pitted dates

¼ cup (30 g) raw, unsalted cashews

2 tablespoons shelled raw walnuts

¼ cup (30 g) shelled unsalted pistachios

4 tablespoons (½ stick/60 g) plant-based butter

¼ cup (21 g) unsweetened dried shredded coconut

Put the pitted dates in a large heatproof mixing bowl and cover with hot water. Soak for 30 minutes to 1 hour to soften.

While the dates are soaking, chop the cashews and walnuts so the pieces are similar in size to the pistachios. Set a large nonstick pan over medium heat and add the pistachios, cashews, and walnuts. Constantly stir them with a spatula, ensuring they evenly toast but do not burn. Toast them for 2 to 3 minutes, until they are lightly browned. Transfer to a plate.

Drain the dates and chop them into small pieces. Add the dates and butter to the same pan and set over medium heat. As the butter melts, stir the date pieces so they are coated in the butter and begin to soften further. Cook the dates for 3 minutes, until they are fragrant, then add the nuts. Stir the dates, butter, and nuts until they are fully mixed and form a homogenous paste. Cook for 2 minutes, until the mixture thickens slightly, then remove the pan from the heat.

(continued)

Transfer the nut and date mixture to a piece of parchment paper and allow it to cool for 10 minutes. Use your hands to form it into a dense log about 1½ inches (4 cm) wide. Spread out the coconut on a wide plate and roll the log in the coconut so it is fully coated. Wrap the log in clean parchment paper and transfer to the fridge for 2 hours to cool and set.

Slice the roll into ½-inch-thick (1 cm) coins. Serve cold or at room temperature.

Store in the fridge in an airtight container for up to 2 weeks.

Resources

Basic items like lentils, tofu, puff pastry, and vegetable oil can be found at most grocery stores, though for the full breadth of lentils, visit your local Indian store. In a pinch, you can use the chickpea flour from Bob's Red Mill as besan. Indian and South Asian markets carry the spices and specialty ingredients you need, and are especially useful for fresh vegetables like okra and mini eggplants. Common Indian brands to look for are MDH (for chunky chaat masala and garam masala), Deep (for lentils and beans), and Anand (for sev and bhel puri mix). Maggi makes a useful spicy ketchup.

For online choices, Diaspora Co. (diasporaco.com) makes small-batch fresh spice options. They also carry tools like a masala dabba for your spices and a tadka spoon. Brightland (brightland.co) has olive oil that is fresh and fragrant.

Here is a list of basics to keep on hand.

Spices
Garam masala
Turmeric, ground
Cumin, ground and seeds
Coriander, ground and seeds
Amchoor (dried mango powder)
Red chili powder
Black mustard seeds
Cardamom pods, green
Kala namak (black salt)

Lentils and Beans
Ahrar daal (pigeon peas)
Masoor daal (red lentils)
Chana (whole chickpeas)
Moong daal (split green lentils)
Urad daal (split black lentils)
Chana daal (split chickpeas)

Grains and Flours
Dalia (cracked wheat)
Sooji (semolina granules)
Poha (flattened rice flakes)
Besan (chickpea flour)
Basmati rice
Atta flour (fine whole wheat flour)

Miscellaneous
Rose water
Rooh afza (rose syrup)
Tamarind concentrate
Masala ketchup
Jaggery
Sev
Bhel puri mix

Acknowledgments

Writing a book was a dream I've always had that I still can't believe has come true. Thank you to series editor Mehreen Karim for thinking of me from the very first day. Thanks to my agent Kitty Cowles for holding my hand every step of the way, and thanks to editorial director Judy Pray for making this book what it became today and for making me a better writer. Abi Balangit, thanks for being the second person I called when I heard about the book and for all your guidance. Andrea Aliseda and Ria Elciario-McKeown, I couldn't have asked for better series authors to go on this journey with!

Emily Eisen, I am lucky to have a friend like you as the creative producer for this series. Tyna Hoang and Andrea Nguyen, my food has never looked as good as when you styled it. Emma Fishman, you really know how to take a beautiful photograph. Sophie Strangio, every prop you chose was perfect. Thanks to Suet Chong for the design of the book. Kimberly Ehart, Analucia Zepeda, and Suzanne Fass, thank you for your infinite patience and attention to detail.

Thank you to everyone who has ever come to a supper club, pop-up, or event. The past few years have been entirely possible because of your support. Thanks to every incredible person who tested recipes; this book would never exist without every single one of you.

I truly believe that I have the most incredible friends in the world. I wish I had space to name everyone, but a lifetime of hugs, help, feedback, and unconditional love is hard to distill. Every friend who has come to dinner, asked about the book, and been a part of my life through this is amazing.

Finally, thanks to my family. Drishaan, you are my best friend. Mom and Dad, I love you; thank you for everything.

Index

R

S

T

W

Y

Z

Srishti Jain is a Californian-Indian food writer, recipe-developer, and vegetarian chef. Growing up in the Bay Area, she began fusing western produce and eastern cuisine from a young age. Throughout her career, her focus has been on expanding her creativity with vegetables and pastry skills. She is known for her supper clubs and pop-ups in San Francisco, New York, London, and beyond as well as her work as a chef at various Brooklyn restaurants. She also writes a newsletter inspiring home chefs to build their own menus and host more dinner parties. She currently resides in Brooklyn with her cat, Clam. Find her @srishti.jpg.